MODELLING ON THE DRESS STAND

Janice Mee and Michael Purdy

BSP PROFESSIONAL BOOKS

OXFORD LONDON EDINBURGH

BOSTON PALO ALTO MELBOURNE

£15.99

The authors wish to thank Graham Tyers for his help
in completing the technical illustrations

First published 1987

British Library
Cataloguing in Publication Data

Mee, Janice
  Modelling on the dress stand.
  1. Dressmaking
  I. Title   II. Purdy, Michael
  646.4'04   TT515

ISBN 0-632-01884-4

BSP Professional Books
Editorial offices:
Osney Mead, Oxford OX2 0EL
  (Orders: Tel. 0865 240201)
8 John Street, London WC1N 2ES
23 Ainslie Place, Edinburgh EH3 6AJ
52 Beacon Street, Boston, Massachusetts 02108, USA
667 Lytton Avenue, Palo Alto, California 94301, USA
107 Barry Street, Carlton, Victoria 3053, Australia

Set by V & M Graphics Ltd, Aylesbury, Bucks
Printed and bound in Great Britain

CONTENTS

1 Introduction   1

2 Modelling – Equipment, Measurement and Preparation   9

3 Skirts   29

4 Bodices   65

5 Necklines   107

6 Collars   113

7 Sleeves   137

8 Draped Styles   157

9 Exercise – A Wedding Dress   181

   Index   187

CHAPTER 1
INTRODUCTION

Draping, toile or modelling on the dress stand as it is more commonly known, is an art and skill which is indispensable to anyone wishing to be successful as a fashion designer. Yet very few books have been written on this subject. Those presently available tend either to be outdated or concerned more with flat-pattern cutting than with the modelling technique.

The authors believe that the importance of mastering this skill cannot be over-emphasised. In order to assist the student or practitioner in developing this skill, the following text has been formulated and structured as an aid for self-instruction, course support, use in designing, designing for individual clients, reference when in practice, designing theatrical costumes, etc. The text covers all aspects of modelling, starting with basic principles and progressing systematically from the simple to the more complicated and extreme applications.

Students of fashion will find the information they need for achieving the necessary standard to complete their professional training. Practitioners will gain information reinforcing that which they already possess, stimulating and encouraging them to use this technique, where in the past they may have omitted to attempt its use in preference for flat-pattern cutting.

What is modelling? As previously indicated, there are three common terms used to describe the technique – *draping, toile* and *modelling*. A fourth term is sometimes used, namely *moulage*. In order that confusion does not reign, it should be realised that these four terms refer to one and the same technique. However, the most modern of these four terms, modelling, is used throughout this book.

Modelling is the moulding of material around a dress stand or human body for the purpose of designing a garment. Just like a sculptor, modelling allows the fashion designer to work in three dimensions. To support the closeness of these two disciplines, history has witnessed the sculptor/fashion designer. For example, Alaia Azzedine was trained as a sculptor but made his career as a couturier. One of his better-known quotes in expressing the value of using modelling for design purposes is: 'I stress the body and I have to try my things on a living body because the clothes I make must respect the body . . .' – a sentiment that is fully supported and expressed in this book.

Before we proceed further with the subject of modelling, it would be prudent to ask what basic skills are needed in order that the techniques described here can be easily and fully understood. The answer to this question is an appreciation of flat-pattern cutting techniques and dressmaking skills. The basic principles of flat-pattern cutting and modelling are similar. Working on the flat in two dimensions is a far simpler concept to master, and once mastered will give students the insight which will allow them to visualise the same pattern in three-dimensions. Although the basic principles of flat-pattern cutting are briefly described later in this chapter, this book in no way attempts to offer in-depth instruction or information on that technique.

Although modelling is basically a skill, artistic acumen is necessary to use the technique to full advantage for the design of a garment. It is for this reason that readers will be guided through the historic development and perspective of modelling.

Artistic acumen is the insight or penetration of the artist into his or her own discipline. Such mastery allows artistic freedom, which in turn, provides the facility for the breaking of rules. It facilitates the creation of innovative designs. No one can predict another's artistic acumen and therefore predict tomorrow's designs. What one can do, however, is look at technological innovation and developing social structures and on that basis predict, in general terms, what demands are likely to be made upon the fashion designer.

BRIEF HISTORIC PERSPECTIVE

Historically, modelling can be seen in two distinct and separate applications – draping cloth around the body to form a garment or draping cloth around a model for the production of a working pattern from which a garment will be cut. We will concern ourselves in the first instance with the draping of skins and cloth around the body as a garment.

If we go back to the time when man recognised the need to cover his body for protection and comfort, the only material available was animal skins. The limited skills available to him then did not include the technology to produce cloth, or the tailoring expertise to make garments. Because of this lack of skill, man found ways of draping these skins around his body. This method of clothing was to remain for many centuries. However, by the time Greek and Roman cultures had developed, a level of sophistication, way beyond that of early man, resulted in draped cloth becoming fashionable garments.

During the time that man used skins as his only form of clothing, there was little change in how these skins were draped. The reason for this would appear to be that animal skins did not allow the variety of size in width and length necessary for experiments in fashion.

Skins continued to be used while tribes were nomadic. Once man began to settle in a given area, developing in terms of permanent abodes, cultivation of land and domestication of animals, his skills, including that of producing cloth, increased. It has been claimed that the various types and designs of loom for the production of cloth reflected the culture of that society in which it was developed. For this reason, it is found that loom widths and lengths of cloth are many and varied.

Seamless garments from loom lengths

Early on in man's cultural evolution, he found that the easiest way of producing a garment was one in which there was no cutting or sewing. In order to do this, pieces of cloth were folded around, draped on or tied to the body. Although this method would appear to have its limitations, in reality that was not so. The Egyptians around the year 2000 BC were producing linen to a loom length of 11 ft (335 cm) and a width of 44" (120 cm). At the same time, they produced a form of pleating, by stretching wet fabric over reeds. When the fabric dried around the reeds, pleats were formed.

The Greek loom could be much wider and they found a method of producing cloth in considerable lengths. The Greek tunic (chiton) which was worn in different lengths, was a loom piece used sideways (Fig. 1.1). There were many ways of draping this material, but in general it was fastened at the shoulders by pins, its shape being adjusted by having an open edge loose down one side, or caught into place, girded around the waist and breasts, allowing the garment to fall into graceful folds. Such forms of dress persisted during the major part of the Greek and Roman Empires. During the cultural development of Roman times, a more specialised form of clothing was developed – the toga (see also Chapter 8). This garment saw the beginning of cut cloth in the forming of clothing. The toga, in its many guises, was not only draped from rectangular pieces, but also from cloth of a circular or hexagonal shape. The hexagon was produced by cutting away the corners of a rectangular piece of cloth or woven to shape. Such a shape allowed for easier and more effective draping.

The sewing of garments

It is not clear when the first sewn garment was produced. Although the Greeks and Romans remained loyal to the simple draping of cloth around the body, it is quite obvious that these societies at some point developed methods of sewing in order to produce garments which would protect their soldiers and merchants while travelling and occupying colder climes. In the main, these garments appear to have been trousers which were worn underneath the draped skirt of the toga. The fashion-concious Romans remained loyal to their opulent and voluminous draped garments, as such garments in their eyes reflected wealth and status. It is not known whether the trousers were sewn or simply pinned.

Upper garments which were not simply draped around the body were being developed. The first and simplest form was a garment similar to the poncho, which was made from a rectangular piece of cloth with a hole in the centre through which the head passed. The lower parts of the sides came together under the arm and were sewn, leaving the upper parts of the sides open to the armholes. This garment was taken a stage further by the ancient Peruvians who added sleeves. They set up a loom to produce four separate lengths and widths – two pieces for the body and two for the sleeves. This, in fact, was an alternative to producing standard widths and lengths from which a garment and its constituent pieces were cut. Obviously, the production of a loom piece to the required size and shape avoided any need to cut.

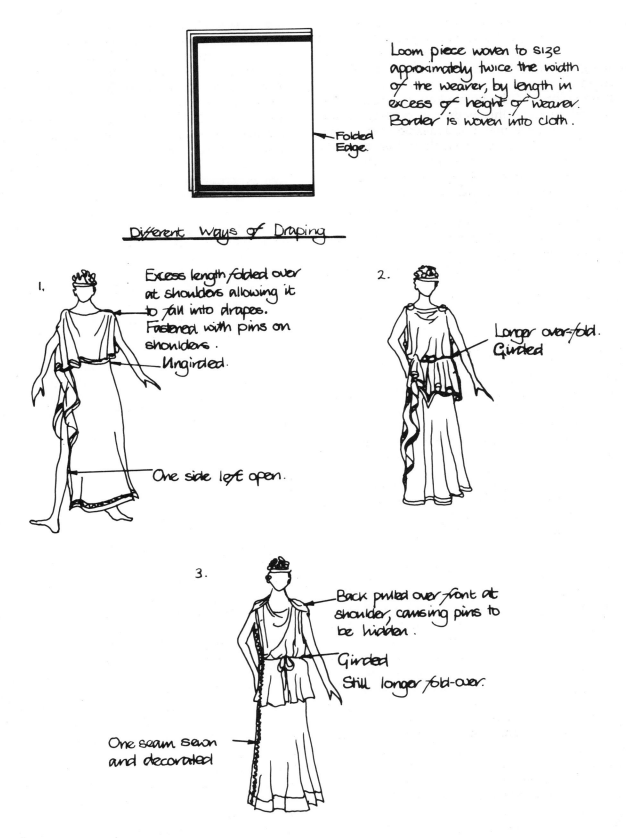

Folded Edge.

Loom piece woven to size approximately twice the width of the weaver, by length in excess of height of weaver. Border is woven into cloth.

Different Ways of Draping

1. Excess length folded over at shoulders allowing it to fall into drapes. Fastened with pins on shoulders.
Ungirded.

One side left open.

2. Longer over-fold. Girded

3. Back pulled over front at shoulder, causing pins to be hidden.
Girded
Still longer fold-over.

One seam sewn and decorated

Fig. 1.1 The Greek chiton.

By weaving to shape, cutting and sewing, societies found that cloth would be saved and that many different functional and fashionable shapes could be produced. Over many decades, this cutting and sewing of cloth became more sophisticated as man developed skills. The skill of cutting and sewing took on a craft, and in many cases, an art form. Clothes being of better shape and, in general terms, size and proportion, became quite complex. This was especially so with those made for the fashionable rich.

It took a great deal of time in fact, right into the Middle Ages, before man developed what we would recognise today as flat pattern cutting. Flat patterns were produced in what many would consider now to be a rough and ready way. The method was one of trial and error, using broad bands of measurements and then adjusting the finished garment to the size and shape of the customer. For the rich, greater accuracy was obtained by fitting a garment to the person by adjustment and then taking a pattern from that garment for future orders for that individual. During this period, mathematical rules were developed for the production of standard sized patterns. The rigidity of the mathematical method was not welcomed by all. Many tailors of the day reverted to their individual, but nevertheless, highly developed methods, effectively disregarding the introduction of standardised sizes.

In England, this position remained much the same until the advent of mechanised sewing in the nineteenth century, when many tailors, in order to gain benefit from factory mass-production, were forced to accept that standardisation was necessary. Although standardisation and mass-production was welcomed by the populace because of the supply of relatively cheap clothing, it did not, of course, satisfy the desires of the higher echelons of society. These people, in order to express their wealth, demanded clothing which was different in both design and manufacture. Many of the better quality dressmakers or tailors had dummies made to a size corresponding to that of their client. This developed to the point where, not only did they fit to the dummy garments which had been originally cut from a flat pattern, but they started cutting the cloth directly on the dummy. This development could arguably be the forerunner to the method which later became known as French draping.

In the middle of the nineteenth century, Charles Frederick Worth, who was working in Paris, began making quality garments, designed and fitted by draping his fabric on individual clients who visited him at his *Maison*. Here we see the beginning of the couture houses. The couturiers quickly discovered that the method of producing a garment from a flat pattern in approximately the right size and then adjusting it to fit the client was not only an expensive and wasteful method but also prevented freedom of design and artistic expression, reducing their effectiveness in producing originality. The couturiers expanded the classical form of dress – the draping of cloth around the body – into a design tool, whereby cloth was draped around a stand of a size compatible to the client. So began, in broad terms, the use of modelling on the stand for the design and production of patterns. This method, being primarily French, was called 'classic French draping' (*moulage*) and has changed little to the present day. It is the primary method used by the majority of *haute couture* designers and increasingly so by the ready-to-wear trade. Later, we shall be looking in greater detail at this method and comparing its applications with flat pattern cutting.

At this stage, it is worth noting that recently the Japanese, who are exerting a great influence upon the fashion world, have adopted modelling but have conceptualised its application in a far different way to the classical traditions.

THE HUMAN BODY AND ITS ARTIFICIAL COVERING

The body has ill-defined boundaries which require protection from the elements. In order to protect itself the body needs some type of armour or shell. Clothing, in addition to its prime function of protecting the body, has other important parts to play in human societies as there is no group of people in the world who are totally unadorned. Body covering performs very important social functions. Naked, there is very little we can tell about one another apart from sexual and age differences. Body condition can also indicate social status but mankind has never been content with such a limited way of socially classifying people. Very early on in the development of the modern world, man discovered that one of the most effective ways of establishing status and social standing was to dress groups within society in accordance with age, function and position. The art of wearing clothes has developed through the ages to a point where the complexity of information given by the wearer can indicate style, taste, status, personality, sexual preference, background, occupation, mood, etc. Such knowledge gained from looking at others conditions the individual in his or her selection of clothing. Being aware of what we see in others, conscious decisions are made about what our new clothing will say and symbolise about us. We all have a mental image of how we wish to look. One of the greatest exponents of images is the advertising industry. The media is highly skilled at presenting us with seductive or reassuring visual displays of people we know or would like to be. In different ways status is interpreted depending upon our own points of reference. Advertising supplies a graphic illustration of how we see ourselves and others.

According to Freud, symbolic messages of our inner selves are displayed in our clothes and our dreams. The modern suit, it has been said, was designed for the physically inactive professional and ruling class. Mass production allowed the working class man to ape his professional counterpart by wearing suits. In order to maintain class barriers and social status, differences are maintained in a more subtle way, mainly in the quality of fabric used in producing the same style of clothing. Almost all styles are self-parodies. The way a peer group dresses could give the impression to an alien that each member of the group is identical. Humans, though, can recognise differences as there are subtleties within each group by which they signal to each other.

To be acceptable to the wearer, clothing must provide protection for the body against the environment, and, in some instances, protection from the body for the environment. Functional aspects are also important, as any restriction upon a body's function will encourage the rejection of a garment. In addition to the physical reactions, psychological comfort must also be provided. Such comfort cannot easily be defined as individuals will differ in how they conceptualise – how they feel, see or react to something that is effectively influencing their environment. Well-defined physical and psychological attributes of clothing are by far the most important influences upon a person as social pressures are, in the main, responsible for what the majority of people wear. Successful designers must temper their artistic desires with physical, psychological and social considerations.

FLAT PATTERN CUTTING

As previously suggested, a prerequisite for understanding modelling as a technique for the production of a garment pattern is a grasp of the basic principles of flat pattern cutting. The information given below on flat pattern cutting techniques is in no way complete as it is the writers' intention simply to supply a broad outline. For greater knowledge of flat pattern cutting, readers are advised to refer to the many excellent books available.

Flat pattern cutting is the mathematical development of a pattern. The technique in its early stages is based upon a two-dimensional conceptualisation of the finished garment. It is only in the latter stages of the pattern development that the designer moves from working on the flat in two dimensions to working in the round in three dimensions.

To make this technique easier to understand, we shall look at the total system of garment production followed when flat pattern cutting is used in preference to modelling as a design tool.

The production of a garment

Fibre

The fibres being produced each year are either those that have been long established and proven successful, or those that have been recently developed and require promotion to test market acceptability. In either case, the fibre manufacturers will decide what fibres they are going to promote in any one season. It must be understood that such a decision is taken at least eighteen months prior to the season in question.

Fabric

Fabric manufacturers will make decisions on the type of weave or knit they are going to use in producing fabric, based upon the type of fibre being supplied to them.

Colour

Colour can be applied to either the fibre before it is woven or knitted, or it can be applied to the fabric.

Finished fabric

It is at this stage that the fashion designer comes on the scene. The designer will be confronted with fabrics of varying textures, weights and colours, made from natural fibres, synthetic fibres or mixtures of both. Generally, the designer working for the couture houses will use high quality fabrics manufactured from natural fibres. Those designers working for mass production units will be confronted with lower quality fabrics produced mainly from synthetic fibres. It should be stated here that the designers working for the couture houses usually have a free choice of fabric, this choice depending on the type of garment they may have already designed on paper, or at the very least, visualised. The opposite is true of the designer working for the mass producer. In some cases, management may have already purchased fabrics in mass quantities at a price which is appropriate to their market outlet, and the designer has to work within the restrictions imposed by those fabrics. No matter what the system of production or the quality of the fabric, we are now at the stage where the designer has to make a decision on which technique to apply in developing a design idea from a sketch to a garment pattern.

The development of the pattern

At this stage, the designers transfer their ideas either from within themselves or from sketches into a pattern form. Although we are concerning ourselves within this chapter with the technique of flat pattern cutting, we cannot avoid reference here to modelling.

A designer working for a couture house and having the monetary backing of such an organisation, would have many lengths of different types and qualities of fabrics to choose from. Many of these fabrics will be catalysts to design ideas. In order to develop the initial, and very often crude design concepts, the designer will take the fabric, handle it, and more often than not, drape it on a model in order to see how the fabric hangs. Following this initial stage, the designer will firm up the design concept, moulding the fabric to the model's contours – this being the beginning of the modelling technique. Alternatively, a designer may design a prototype, produce toiles, and then choose fabric to suit the design.

Designers working in the mass market may have a fabric they are to use at hand and will be in no position to reject it in preference for another. In addition to this restriction, the clothing manufacturer, for whom they work and who is supplying the mass market, will have developed standard lines over the years. The designer will be employed mainly for the purpose of turning these standard lines into garments reflecting present day fashions. Such changes can be quite superficial and easily assimilated visually in two dimensions. It is, therefore, very often the case that designers, working in the mass-production field, will convert their ideas in sketch form to pattern form using the two-dimensional flat pattern cutting technique. This does not mean that designers who have little, if any, choice as to the selection of fabric do not use modelling in order to develop their design concepts. They often do, but, unlike the couture house designer, they are faced with the problem of fabrics and standard line designs which for the mass market require what is referred to as 'hanger appeal'. This term refers to what a garment looks like on a hanger in a high street shop. Many draped styles, even of the highest quality, do not hang well when off the body. The test of such appeal in the mass market means a reduction in sales. Hanger appeal is obtained by manufacturers having, over the years, developed and built into their standard lines a cut of garment giving this quality. This cut is maintained by the use of standard blocks on to which the present fashion trend is interpreted. Such restrictions, and that is what they are to the designer, tend to encourage the use of flat pattern cutting as against modelling.

Flat pattern cutting method

A garment pattern is produced from a design sketch. The technique uses a mathematical base, requiring figures in the form of measurements. Such measurements are obtained either from existing statistical data, representing a range of average measurements of a particular population (such data obviously changes depending upon its ethnic base) or are taken directly from the body or dress stand. Such measurements are expressed as lengths or widths no matter what their origin. Basic garment shapes – for example, a bodice or a sleeve – will be produced in card using these measurements. These pieces of card are referred to as the blocks.

The block

A block is a basic outline of a part of a garment. The measurements taken as described above would be adjusted upwards to allow for movement, i.e. to allow the body space within the garment. The exception to an increase in measurement is where certain types of knitwear or stretch fabrics are used, then very often the nett measurement is reduced to allow for the extension built into the fabric. Once the measurement has been established it is transferred on to card where the total measurements taken will produce an outline shape of part of a garment. The card is cut to this outline, thus producing a block. A set of such blocks put together and often pinned on to a stand will represent the total garment. The fit of the blocks to the stand needs to be accurate and any adjustments to the blocks can be seen at this stage. These blocks can be made to either individual or standard statistical measurements. In order to check the accuracy of the blocks, they are often transferred onto muslin which is then fitted to the stand to make sure that the block can be interpreted in terms of fabric.

These blocks are called *primary blocks*. To produce more complex shapes such as a raglan sleeve block, the primary blocks of sleeve and bodice are placed together and the raglan sleeve line drawn over the two. From this a *secondary block* is produced. So that fit can be obtained, especially on the female form, darts are introduced on to the block.

There are two systems that can be used for drafting out a basic block. The first is referred to as *divisional* or *proportional* and the second as *direct drafting*. The titles are self-explanatory in that the first uses standard measurements representative of a particular population, whereas the second uses measurements taken from an individual or stand. The designer working for a mass production unit, would usually find that the company would have their own standard set of blocks. These blocks would be representative of the type of style of garment which the company usually produced and also the fit of garment in relation to the population they supplied. This means, of course, that the designer would not have to produce a block, whereas the couture house designer most probably would.

Garment patterns

Once the block has been made or chosen from a company's stock it is traced on to paper. This paper, being the working draft, is pinned on to the stand and the details of the garment to be produced are added to it. Such details would include collars, style lines, etc. The draft is then removed from the stand and any adjustments necessary are made on the flat. From this draft, the garment pattern is produced on paper. From this paper pattern, a sample garment is made and tried on a live model. If the sample is successful, then a production pattern in card is made.

CHAPTER 2
MODELLING – EQUIPMENT, MEASUREMENT AND PREPARATION

Modelling is the moulding of fabric around a dress stand or live model in order to create a garment. This method has two distinct advantages, the first being that the designer is working in three dimensions which assists a total understanding of the appearance of the finished garment. Secondly, it can allow the designer to work in factual measurements as against statistical data. Such an approach is so free of general rules that it allows complete freedom of expression, evolving through experimentation. On the other hand, there are enough rules if one wishes to implement them for analytical and systematic development.

SELECTING EQUIPMENT

It is important for a designer or, for that matter, anyone pursuing a craft to acquire equipment that is correct and of a quality which will not obstruct the development of that for which it is to be used.

Dress stand
Dress stands represent both the size and shape of a human torso. They are available in a wide range of sizes and shapes. A standard shape is one that complies to fixed sizes, e.g. size 10, 12, 14, 16, together with the fashionable proportion to those sizes. In addition to these standard sizes, speciality stands for designing coats, trousers, childrenswear etc., can be obtained. No one dress stand is ideal for all needs, although adjustments can be made to a stand by padding for particular purposes. Adjustable stands are available but as yet have proved to be unsuccessful because the degree of adjustment available within any part of the stand is not extensive enough.

Stands, in general terms, reflect present day fashionable shape and proportion. Change in shape and proportion tends only to be made if a drastic move in fashionable size and shape takes place.

When selecting a dress stand, it is advisable to choose one which is covered in canvas and seamed. These seams are positioned at the centre front, centre back, sides, shoulders, neck and waistline. There are demarcation lines from shoulder through bust point and waist to end of torso, and from the shoulder, at the same point, down the back, through the waist to the end of the torso. These lines are used for establishing the position of darts and seams (see Fig. 2.18).

Whatever type of stand is chosen, it is important that it is attached to a firm base providing stability. It is advisable to have castors on the base to allow for ease of movement. Two adjustments should be available, one being the height and the second the shoulders. Their importance will be recognised later. Some stands have a wire cage below the torso which assists in the modelling of long skirts. The selection of a good quality stand will allow for many adjustments to be made by adding parts such as arms, for example.

Cutting table
The ideal table is one which is approximately 3 metres long and 1.5 metres wide and of a height which is comfortable to the user. Its surface should not be too hard or slippery, providing some friction between it and the fabric.

Mirror
It is desirable to have a full-length mirror high enough to cover the height of the stand and any live model used, and low enough to show the feet at the same time. Its width should be such that both sides of the garment are visible. It should be understood here that many garments, especially skirts, could be much wider than the stand.

Steam iron and board
Any steam iron with a well defined point is suitable. A standard board including a sleeve board is also required.

Scissors and shears
Good quality cutting equipment is imperative. A minimum of two pairs of shears is required, one for cutting paper, the other for fabric. At least one small pair of scissors for nicking, unpicking and cutting ends of threads is needed.

'L' square
Two are required.

Set square
One 150 mm (6") 45° set square.

Tracing wheel
Choose one with long spikes.

Tape measure
A dual-purpose dressmaker's tape measure is required with metric measurements on one side and imperial on the other.

Rules
Two rules are required, one being a metre stick and the other a short rule. (Imperial scale is desirable on the opposite edge to the metric scale.)

Unpicker
One required.

Weights
Any form of weights can be used, as long as they are heavy enough to prevent the fabric moving on the cutting table. These weights should be made of material which will not damage the fabric, and their size and shape must not obstruct the cutting process.

Pins
Fine and long. Silk pins for draping.

Tailor's chalk
Dark for marking light coloured fabric and light for marking dark coloured fabric.

Paper
Pattern cutting paper which can be either plain white or spot and cross, which assists in establishing dimensions and grain lines.

Card
Pattern card.

Pencils
Hard, at least 2H, which provides fineness of line. Soft pencils are also needed for marking muslin.

Black tape
6 mm (¼") in width.
Plain black non-stretchable fabric tape.

Sellotape
12 mm (½") – 18 mm (¾") in width.

Wadding
Dressmaker's poly wadding.

The equipment listed above is essential. In addition, in order to make life easy, it is desirable that pattern notches, a wrist pin cushion, french curves, an apron with a large front pocket, pattern hooks, and a hole punch are obtained.

MEASUREMENTS

Measurements will be obtained in one of two ways. If we are designing for the individual, then measurements will be taken from that individual's body. If we are not designing for the individual, then those measurements representing a standard size 12 will be used (see *Fig. 2.1* for the standard body measurements chart). In either case, these sets of measurements will be represented on the stand. Accurate representation for non-standard measurements, i.e. those taken from the individual, is obtained by padding the stand.

TAKING BODY MEASUREMENTS

When taking body measurements, standardisation is important, so that the designer is always working from the same base. To obtain standardisation and accuracy, a check list, in the form of a chart, should be drawn up as illustrated below. The check list (Fig. 2.2) is representative of that used by the majority of designers. Some designers choose to take different measurements and in effect establish their own standard measurements. Such an approach is fine, as long as these measurements generally remain constant. Specialist measurements for specialist garments can, and are, added to standard lists.

Part of body	Measurements cm (in)		
	Size 10	Size 12	Size 14
Bust	81 (32)	86.5 (34)	91.5 (36)
Waist	61 (24)	66 (26)	71 (28)
Hips	86.5 (34)	91.5 (36)	96.5 (38)
Centre back neck to waist	39 (15⅜)	39.5 (15½)	40 (15¾)
Front shoulder to waist	38.5 (15¼)	39.5 (15½)	40.5 (16)
Full length skirt from waist	101.5 (40)	103 (40½)	104 (41)
Waist to knee	59.5 (23½)	61 (24)	62 (24½)
Back width	33 (13)	34 (13½)	35.5 (14)
Chest width	35.5 (14)	37 (14½)	38 (15)
Shoulder length	12.5 (5)	12.5 (5)	13 (5¼)
Neck	7 (2¾)	7.25 (2⅞)	7.5 (3)
Depth of scye	20 (8)	21 (8¼)	21.5 (8½)
Length of arm	57 (22½)	58 (22¾)	58.5 (23)
Top arm width	28 (11)	29 (11½)	30.5 (12)
Wrist width	15.5 (6)	16 (6¼)	16.5 (6½)

Fig. 2.1 Standard body measurements chart.

Parts of the body	Figure measurements	Stand measurements	Discrepancies
Bust			
Waist			
Hips			
Centre back neck to waist			
Front shoulder to waist			
Back width			
Chest width			
Shoulder length			
Neck			
Depth of scye			
Length of arm			
Top arm width			
Elbow width			
Wrist width			
Full length from waist			
Waist to knee (crutch depth) (body rise)			
Width and thickness of bust			
Width and thickness of hips			
Body rise			

Fig. 2.2 Comparative measurement chart.

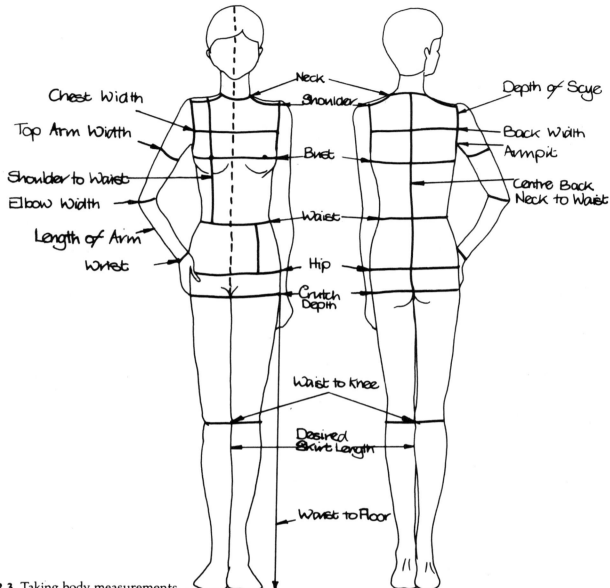

Fig. 2.3 Taking body measurements.

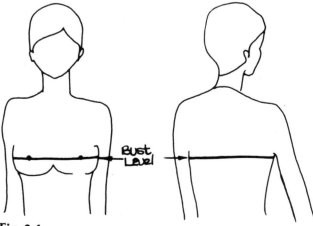

Fig. 2.4

Measurements on the female form (Fig. 2.3) should be taken with the person in brassiere and pants standing in relaxed position. When measuring the arm it should be bent with hand resting on hip.

Bust

Fig. 2.4
Measure round the fullest part of the bust, keeping the tape measure raised slightly at the back, just below the shoulder blades.

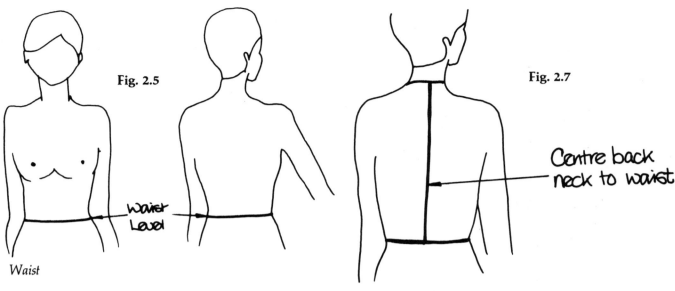

Waist

Fig. 2.5
Measure around the natural waist, firmly but not tightly. Secure tape around the waist in preparation for taking any vertical measurements from that point.

Centre back neck to waist

Fig. 2.7
Measure from the top cervical bone at the back of the neck to the bottom of the waist tape.

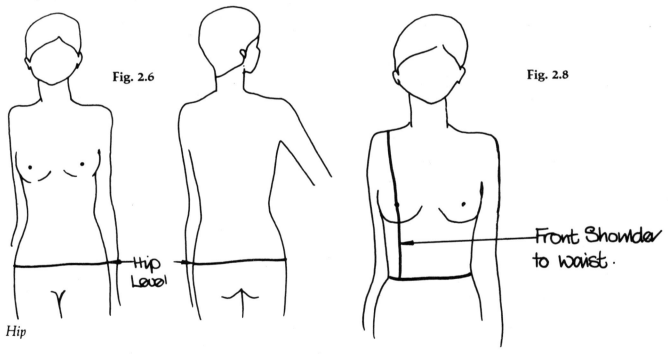

Hip

Fig. 2.6
This circumferential measurement is normally taken 200 mm (8″) – 225 mm (9″) down from the waist tape. The latitude allowed between the two measurements is to account for variance in the height of the figure. Always measure round the fullest part fairly tightly with the figure standing with feet together.

Front shoulder to waist

Fig. 2.8
Take the measurement from the centre of the shoulder, over the apex of the bust to the bottom of the waist tape. (This measurement is sometimes taken from the neckpoint on the shoulder.)

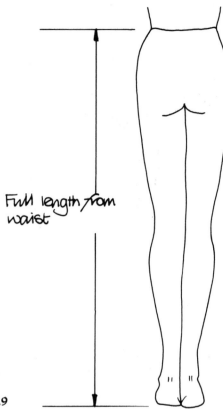

Full length from waist

Fig. 2.9
Measure from bottom of waist tape to the floor, centre back, centre front and sides in order to check that the balance is even.

Fig. 2.9

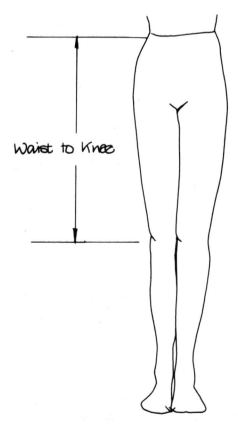

Waist to knee

Fig. 2.10
Measure from the bottom of the waist tape to where the knee bends.

Fig. 2.10

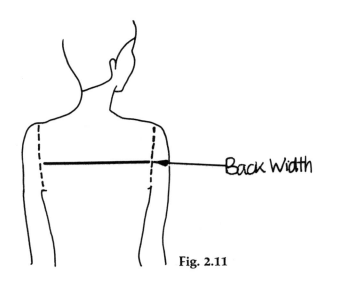

Fig. 2.11

Back width

Fig. 2.11
Take this measurement with the figure in its normal stance. Measure from armhole to armhole approximately 100 mm (4″) below the top cervical vertebra.

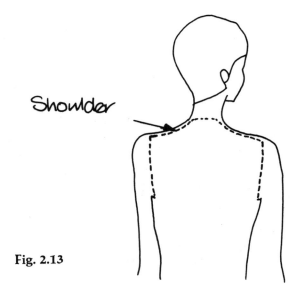

Fig. 2.13

Shoulder length

Fig. 2.13
Measure along the top of the shoulder from the neck point to the most prominent point of the shoulder bone.

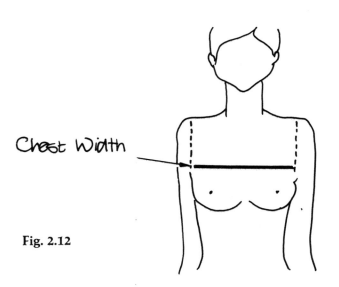

Fig. 2.12

Chest width

Fig. 2.12
This is taken approximately 75 mm (3″) down from the top notch of the sternum at the centre front across from armhole to armhole.

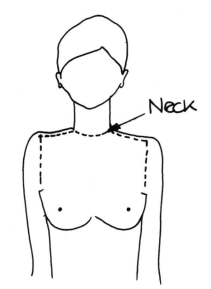

Fig. 2.14

Neck

Fig. 2.14
Take the measurement around the base of the neck, or the seam line on the dress stand.

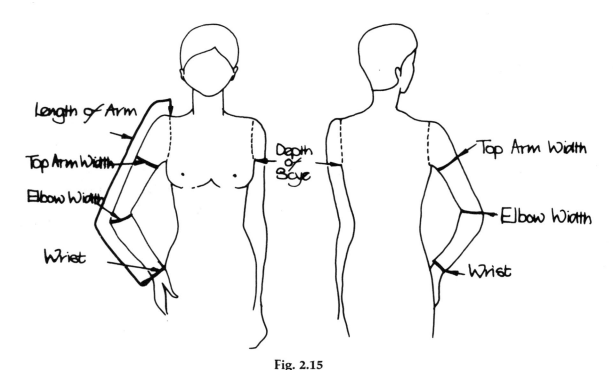

Fig. 2.15

Fig. 2.15
Elbow width
Keeping the arm in the same position, measure round the elbow over the elbow point.

Depth of scye
This is the depth of armhole and the measurement should be taken from the shoulder point 37 mm (1½″) down from the armpit with the arm in an extended position.

Length of arm
Have the hand resting on the hip and take the measurement of the arm, from the shoulder point, over the elbow to the wrist bone in line with the little finger.

Top arm width
Keeping the arm in the same position, measure round the fullest part of the arm (biceps).

Wrist
Measure through wrist bones.

Body rise (sometimes called crutch depth)

Fig. 2.16
This is taken to allow for the garment rising on the seated figure.
Measure the figure in a seated position down the side of the body from the taped waist to the seat level.

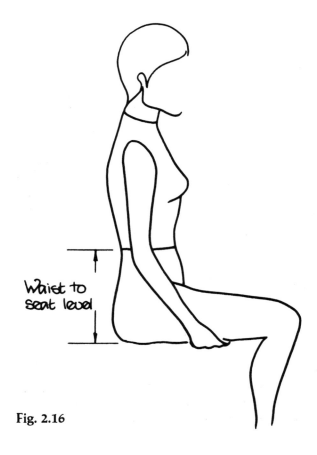

Fig. 2.16

Widths and thicknesses

Fig. 2.17

Bust
Bust width is obtained by placing the subject with her back to the wall. Position two squares with the short arm against the wall so that the long arm touches the side of each breast. The distance between the two projecting squares is bust width. *Bust depth* is obtained by retaining the two squares in position and placing a rule aross the top of the projecting square arms, just touching the most prominent point of the bust. The distance from the rule to the wall is the bust depth.

Hips
Width and depth are obtained by using the same method.

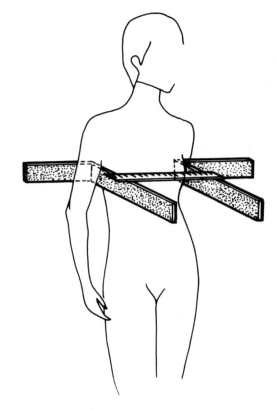

Fig. 2.17 Widths and thicknesses.

TRANSFERRING BODY MEASUREMENTS ONTO THE STAND

The nett measurements we now possess on our comparative measurement chart have to be transferred in working sizes on to the stand. What is meant by working sizes? By way of explanation, let us look at what those measurements found on a standard size 12 stand represent.

A size 12 garment is made to fit a body measuring 87 cms (34″) bust, 64 cms (25″) waist and 92 cms (36″) hips. If the garment was made exactly to these sizes, then the wearer would have no room within for body movement and function. To facilitate body movement and function, nett measurements have to be increased, this increase being referred to as *tolerance*. The amount of tolerance depends upon the shape and design of the garment, the type of material in which it is to be made, and the purpose for which the garment is being worn.

Let us take each of the three factors affecting tolerance and investigate them separately.

Shape and design of the garment

Shape and design are a reflection of current fashionable trends. In extreme cases, the fashionable trend may well dictate that the tolerance for movement allowed within a garment should be negligible, often to the point of creating discomfort for the wearer. Putting such difficulties to one side, the designer should attempt to allow enough tolerance within the shape and design of the garment to allow for it to be worn comfortably. The design skill is in providing the tolerance necessary while at the same time creating the 'Look' that the design demands.

Material

Looking once again at extremes, we have fabrics that will stretch and mould themselves to body shape and fabrics which have little give in them. A close-fitting knitted garment, or one in stretch fabric will require little, if any, tolerance. Stretch fabric could demand a reduction in garment size below the nett body measurement in order to emphasise the quality of stretch when worn. In such cases, it is clear that a stand, which is smaller than the nett body sizes, must be used, so that it can be padded up to the size required for the fabric. At the other end of the scale, if you were producing a suit of armour, which is effectively in a material with no practical give, then a large tolerance would have to be built into the nett measurements.

The purpose for which the garment is being worn

Specialist garments often require tolerances different from those allowed for everyday wear. Such garments are those which may be worn for particular types of employment, sporting activity, etc. Tolerance in such instances can be provided either within the garment, or in the fabric from which the garment is to be made. Much data is available which will indicate the amount of tolerance required for such garments. If such data is not adequate, then simple experiments with the subject wearing prototype garments would furnish the information required.

Having now considered these points, and knowing what material you intend to use, you must decide what tolerances you will allow in all areas of the body on your nett measurements. The nett measurements together with the tolerance equals the figure measurement which you should enter under that column on your chart.

You now measure your stand, entering the measurements on your chart in the relevant column. On completion of the stand measurement column, read across the chart and the difference, if any, between stand and figure measurements should be entered in the column entitled 'discrepancies'.

A designer requires, at all times, to have the maximum amount of information available. In many respects, raw measurements on a chart, although accurate, require quantifying descriptively. It is therefore necessary that any information concerning the individual you have measured, which will affect the garment to be made, should be entered alongside those measurements in the discrepancies column. As an example, it may be that the person measured has prominent shoulder blades, or a body which is totally out of symmetry.

The chart, when completed, will contain that information which will allow us to start work on padding the stand. If no differences or information is recorded in the discrepancy column, this will indicate that the stand is already representative of the body and does not require padding.

PADDING A STAND

Let us assume that we have a great deal of information in our discrepancies column.

You should select a stand which is as small as the least of the three main width measurements: bust, waist and hips. The stand should also have a length from centre back neck to waist which is as close as possible to that measurement recorded on your chart. You should recognise that this length measurement is important, as it cannot be altered on the stand, whereas we can use padding to alter width measurements.

Padding procedure

Padding is used to build up those areas of a stand which are smaller in dimension than the size of the garment required. Do not attempt to build up isolated areas with one thickness of wadding. Gradually develop thickness from a point of zero on the stand's surface, working in thin layers of wadding, to that part of the stand where the maximum depth of padding is required. Continuous and even graduation of line on the padded surface must be achieved. These layers of wadding are obtained by splitting and teasing out layers from the manufacturer's length. The first layer of wadding should be pinned firmly, sinking the pins into the stand. Each succeeding layer of wadding will adhere to the previous layer and should not require pinning. Working towards the point of maximum thickness, smooth the cut edges of the wadding into the preceding layer, forming a continuous contour. In some instances, it may be found that, for example, the whole of the stand for the bodice requires padding. In such cases, it is easier if a single piece of wadding, covering the whole of the bodice, is used as the base layer. As this wadding is moulded around the contour of the stand, excess wadding in areas of supression, should be snipped away to the apex, e.g. bust point or point of shoulder blade. Once the stand is covered with this base piece of wadding, the procedure for padding, described above, is followed.

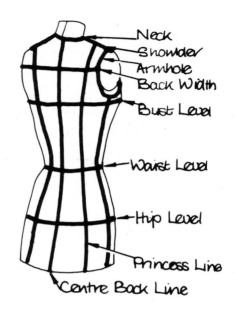

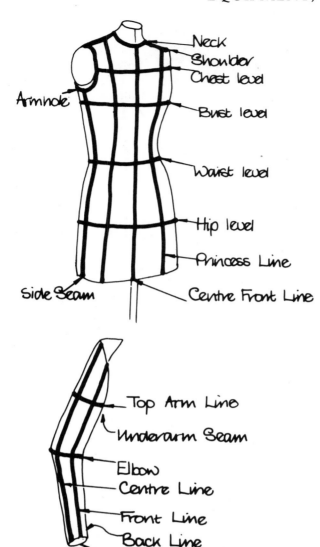

Fig. 2.18 Taping a dress stand for a block.

Wadding will not always provide the necessary effect and other materials can be used in such cases. A good example is where a stand does not have the width of shoulder required. Card cut into semicircles with the straight edge towards the neck and pinned down to the shoulders will provide the width you require. A similar technique can be used below the torso, so that a long skirt can be modelled.

Having padded the stand, check all measurements against those recorded on your chart. In addition to the check on measurements, ensure that the figure shape including stance and general overall proportion reflects those comments made in your discrepancies column.

TAPING A DRESS STAND

Taping a dress stand can be done in one of two ways. The first method is used for taping the stand in order to produce a *block*. The second is used for taping to produce a *style*.

Taping for the production of a block

The tape on a stand provides two functional purposes. The first is that the tape will hold the padding firm and the second is that the tape position will provide demarcation lines necessary for the positioning of the seams, darts, drapes, yokes, pockets, collars etc. Note that an unpadded stand will have many of these lines indicated by surface seams. Black stay tapes should be used to provide the firmness required and the colour necessary to see where they are located through the stand cover. (The stand cover will be made later.)

Demarcation lines

Figure 2.18 shows all the taped lines required for the production of a block. The position of these lines are in accordance with those measurements and rules described previously in this chapter in the section concerned with body measurements. The exception to this is the position of the tape for the armhole. The tape starts at the shoulder point, curving inwards to the chest line. This is the

Fig. 2.19 Taping a dress stand for a style.

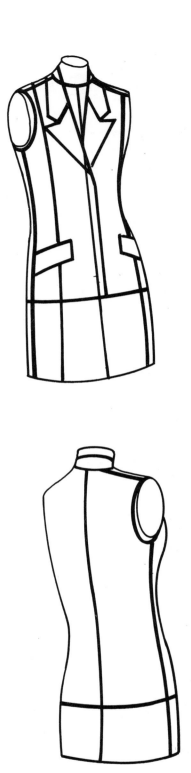

deepest point of the curve. It then moves outwards in a smooth arc to the underarm seam. The depth of the scye is approximately 19 cms (7½"). Keep the curve approximately 1.5 cms (⅝") away from the armhole contour of the stand. This curve can be checked against a good standard block. If seam lines on the original stand are visible at the perimeters of padding, then these should be followed.

Taping the stand for a style

Demarcation lines for a style will obviously follow the design features. When taping for a style, it is necessary to tape the whole stand to ensure that the design is balanced and in good proportion. An example of taping for a style is shown in Fig. 2.19.

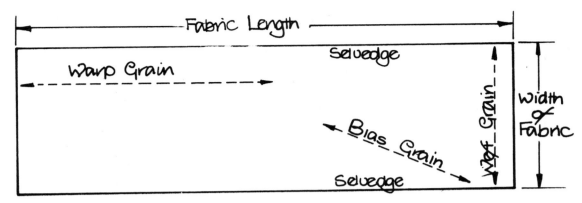

Fig. 2.20 Grain lines.

FABRIC FOR MODELLING

The fabric chosen for modelling should resemble as closely as possible the fabric in which the garment will be made. Some couturiers will model in the fabric itself, but of course this is very expensive. In the wholesale trade, it is customary to use a similar cloth which is less expensive, or a piece left over from a previous collection. Draped styles should be modelled in the actual garment cloth whenever possible, as the fabric will influence the design.

For constructing basic shapes, muslin or calico are the best fabrics to use. They can be purchased in several different weights:

- Light-weight – good for soft draping.
- Medium-weight, coarsely woven – good for styles of garments which are neither light-weight nor heavy-weight.
- Heavy-weight, firmly woven – ideal for tailored garments.

Whichever is selected, the main requirements are that the fabric for a foundation block should have a definite grain line and be transparent enough to see the black tape lines beneath it on the stand. When the cover is pulled over the stand, the fabric needs to be firm enough to withstand any stretching, whilst being sufficiently pliable for pins to be inserted. Finally, it should mould easily to the contours of the body or stand.

Grain lines

If the grain lines (see Fig. 2.20) are ignored, the garment will not hang correctly when it is placed on a stand or figure. It is therefore important to understand the effect grain has on a garment.

The directions in which the fibres lie is referred to as the grain. These directions may be the warp grain or the weft grain.

The warp grain

The warp grain runs parallel to the selvedge, i.e. length-wise down a piece of material. It is the strongest and has the least amount of stretch of the grains. For this reason, it is normally placed down the centre front and back of garments and down the centre of sleeves.

The weft grain

The weft grain runs from selvedge to selvedge across the width of fabric. It is weaker than the warp grain, but possesses slightly more stretch.

The bias grain

The bias grain (see Fig. 2.21) causes the garment to cling to the body and produces the best drapes. If the design requires a figure-hugging silhouette, then the bias grain should be placed down the centre front and back. To give a rolled effect on a collar, the top collar should be placed on the bias, mounted on an under collar with a straight grain.

This grain is not the result of the direction of fibres in the manufactured fabric. It is obtained in the making of the garment, by placing the fabric at an angle to the pattern. Any angle can be used in isolation to obtain design features, but an angle of 45° is required to produce the 'true bias' and a symmetrical garment.

If fabric is used on the bias, then you are effectively introducing a weakness and the fabric

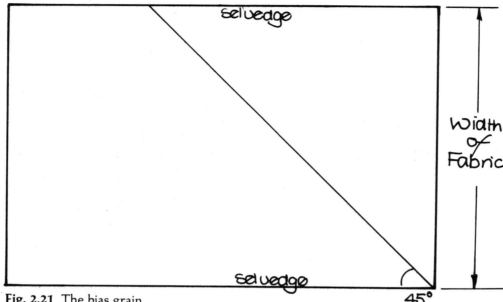

Fig. 2.21 The bias grain.

will tend to drop. It is advisable to hang the garment for as long as possible before levelling the hemline.

Preparation of the fabric

Before modelling, the muslin or calico needs some preparation.

1.   Estimate the amount of fabric required, taking into account the extra needed for the contours of the body, styling, seam allowances and movement.

2.   Do not cut across the width, but tear, after nicking into the edge with shears. This breaks the threads and will run along the weft grain. (Knitted fabrics and fabrics which fray easily will have to be cut.)

3.   Since the selvedge is more tightly woven than the rest of the material, it is best to cut it off as it tends to hold in the fabric and causes seams to pucker.

4.   Often the fabric is 'off grain', i.e. the weft threads are not at right angles to the warp threads. To rectify this it is necessary to 'block' the fabric by pulling diagonally across it until it is corrected. The fabric is then steam-pressed followed by a dry iron, without pressing on the bias.

The balance of the garment depends upon having the weft grain square to the warp grain when modelling the basic blocks. In the bodice, the weft grain should be square to the centre across the bust line; in the skirt, it should be square to the centre across the hip line and, in the sleeve, the top arm line should be square to the centre vertical line.

We have now reached the stage where we are ready to start modelling. In your possession you have all the tools and equipment including a prepared stand and fabric.

MODELLING THE STAND COVER/ BASIC BLOCK (PRINCESS LINE)

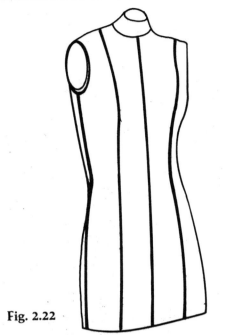

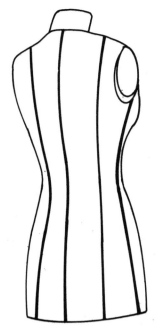

Fig. 2.22

As well as being used to make the cover for a stand that has been padded, the block made from the toile can be used as a foundation block for flat pattern cutting purposes. It must be accurate in order to show any mistakes in the modelling or padding. It should be void of wrinkles or drag lines and should fit the stand with no extra movement.

The princess line

The princess line is ideal for fitting purposes and has eight vertical panels (Fig. 2.22).

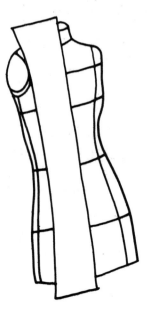

Fig. 2.23 The stand cover basic block (princess line).

Preparing the material

Fig. 2.23
Select a material suitable as previously described for covering the padded and taped stand. Prepare the material as previously described.

Before you cut your material, consider the measurement data you have in your possession. If the data shows that the figure is symmetric then you will be covering only one half of each part of the stand, that half being the right hand side. If the figure is out of symmetry, then it is wise to cover the whole of the stand.

Follow the instructions, assuming that we have a symmetrical figure.

Centre front panel

Fig. 2.24

Place the warp grain of the muslin along the middle of the tape centre front line allowing enough material for the height of the shoulders and the depth of the torso. Pin down the centre front at the neck, chest, bust, waist, hips and base.

Keeping the weft grain at right angles to the warp grain, smooth the fabric out towards the bust point and pin on to the apex. Do the same on the hip and base lines.

Before we proceed further, knowledge of pinning technique is required.

Pinning

Since the pinned muslin represents the final garment, seam allowances and darts should be turned under with the pins approximately 2.5 cms (1") to 5 cms (2") apart (dependent upon how close-fitting the style is). These pins should be positioned at right angles to the seams. Normally, each pin is pushed into the stand and out again, picking up approximately ½ cm (¼") to 1 cm (½") of material.

One exception to this is if you are working in a small area, e.g. a collar (Fig. 2.25), and you do not wish to disguise a line; then the pin is pushed straight into the stand. Another exception is if you are pinning pleats or holding a sleeve onto the stand (Fig. 2.26). In an instance, such as the latter, or if the garment is not tight-fitting, then pin to the stand as little as possible to allow the fabric to hang as it would do on a figure.

When taping a stand the pins should be sunk into the stand right up to the head. The number of pins used should be just enough to hold the taped lines securely to the stand so that they do not move.

When draping, all details should be marked with pins which should lie in the direction of any seams, darts, tucks and folds etc.

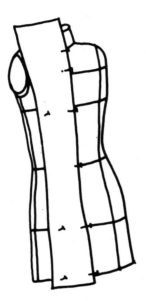

Fig. 2.24 Centre front panel.

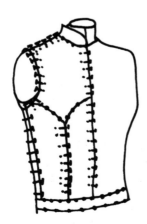

Fig. 2.25

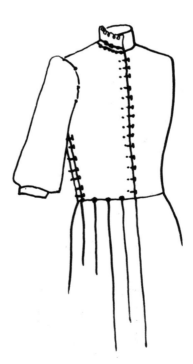

Fig. 2.26

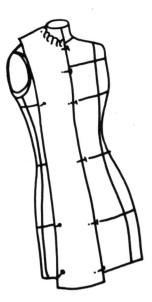

Pinning the centre front panel

Fig. 2.27
From the centre front neck, smooth the muslin away round the neck and towards the shoulder, pinning on to the taped line and cutting away the surplus muslin to within 1 cm (½") of the neck. Nick into the neckline so that the fabric will lie smoothly round the taped line.

Fig. 2.27

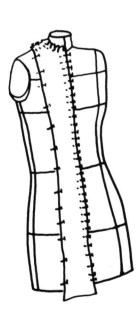

Fig. 2.28
Fill in pins down centre front between neck, chest, bust, waist, hips and base at approximately 5 cms (2") intervals.

Smooth the fabric out from the centre front and up towards the shoulder. Pin onto taped shoulder line and cut away surplus to within 2 cms (¾").

Pin down the princess style line from shoulder to base, making sure the weft grain is kept at right angles to the centre front line at bust, hip and base levels.

Cut away surplus fabric to within 2 cms (¾"), nicking into the seam at waist level.

Fig. 2.28

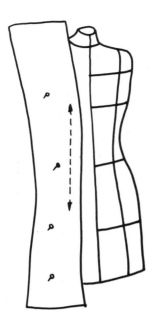

Fig. 2.29

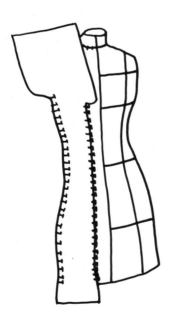

Fig. 2.30

Side front panel

Fig. 2.29
Cut fabric, allowing for seams and body contours to a width size between princess and side seam lines and length size to cover torso.

Place the fabric on the side panel of the stand with the warp grains running parallel to the centre front.

Pin the centre of the panel at waist, armhole, hip and base level.

Fig. 2.30
Smooth fabric onto side seam from pinned points. Pin and cut away surplus fabric to within 2 cms (¾") and nick into seams at waist curve.

Repeat the operation, smoothing fabric towards the princess line as far as bust level.

Fig. 2.31
Smooth the fabric above the bust level inwards and upwards towards the princess style line from the armhole. Smooth, pin and cut away the surplus fabric to within 1 cm (½"), nicking into the curved seam allowance. On reaching the shoulder point, pin along the shoulder line and cut away the surplus fabric to within 2 cms (¾").

Release the pins from the princess style line seam and turn the seam allowances back onto the side panel.

Remove the temporary pins from the centre of the side panel and any other unnecessary ones.

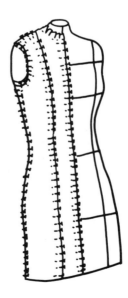

Fig. 2.31

Back princess line foundation cover

Follow the same procedure as for the front. The difference is that the ease is around the shoulder blade position instead of the bust. The seam between the centre back panel and the side back panel is turned towards the side back panel.

The side seam is turned towards the side back panel.

When completed, all seams should be turned inwards with all sections touching.

With a pencil, mark the muslin along the seam to the centre of the taped seam lines on the stand. Indicate balance marks. A balance mark is usually indicated where a change in contour occurs, or easing in is necessary. Mark the grain line on each section (Fig. 2.32). Mark in neckline, armhole and hemline.

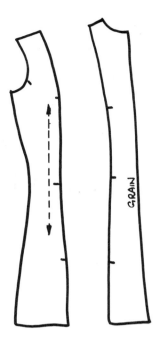

Fig. 2.32

Removal of muslin pieces (toile) from the stand

The panels should be taken off the stand carefully, as the mere handling of fabric can stretch it. Remove all pins, starting at the lowest point. Lay one piece at a time on the ironing board and pin down without stretching or causing any distortion. Press carefully with a dry iron. Remove from ironing board and place onto a white or spot and cross paper and weigh down.

Now your muslin is on the flat, discrepancies of line can be observed. These should be corrected ('trueing'). With a tracing wheel, trace the outline, interior details, grain lines and balance marks onto the paper. From the traced outline, measure and mark the required seam allowances.

When all lines have been marked cut the paper following outlines inclusive of seam allowances of each panel. These are your pattern pieces.

This same procedure is followed for any style and if going into production the following information is required on each piece of pattern:
(1)　Name of piece.
(2)　Number of pieces required.
(3)　Warp grain line.
(4)　Balance marks.
(5)　Any necessary details, e.g. pocket position if a style has been produced.
(6)　Style number.
(7)　Size.

A paper pattern is not necessary if the garment is a 'one-off'.

In this instance, we are going to produce a complete cover for the stand.

Cover for the stand

Spread a new piece of muslin out on your work table. Lay the pattern pieces on the muslin, placing them as closely as possible to each other to reduce wastage of material. Ensure that the pattern pieces are positioned with their marked warp grain line corresponding to the warp grain line in the fabric.

When your pattern pieces are correctly positioned, weigh down and mark outlines with either pencil or chalk.

Remove pattern pieces. Cut muslin following outline marks.

On each piece indicate detail e.g. balance marks.

Now make up, leaving back seam undone.

Place stand in front of a full length mirror.

Put cover on stand, pinning up the back seam.

In the mirror, observe the overall view. Look for drag lines, wrinkles and bulges. Ensure that seams are in line with taped seam lines on stand.

The hang

Centre front, centre back and side seams are the vertical balance lines viewed face on, and should be perpendicular.

Bust and hip levels, being the horizontal balance lines viewed face on, should be at right angles to the vertical balance lines.

Drag lines, wrinkles and bulges

If there are any drag lines, wrinkles or bulges, the possible cause would be in incorrect pattern pieces or material being distorted in preparation.

When everything is correct, sew up the back seam. You now have a stand cover ready for modelling and pattern pieces forming your basic block.

CHAPTER 3
SKIRTS

In this chapter, a number of styles of skirts will be illustrated. In the following chapters, different styles of bodices, necklines and collars, sleeves and draperies will also be set out. All these styles have been chosen to represent a broad range. It should be noted that classic styles are used, but the basic principles apply irrespective of the fashion of the day.

In this and the following chapters, the first example of the procedure to be followed will be detailed and fully illustrated. All subsequent examples shall have only that detailed information which is not given in the first example.

At this stage, a decision has to be made about what approach you wish to take in producing your garment. If you wish to produce a number of garments of the same style, you will need to make a pattern from the toile. If your intention is to produce one garment only, then a pattern will not be required and you can do one of two things. The first is to model the garment on the stand in a cheaper material. Once the toile is completed to your satisfaction, you go on to produce your garment by using it as a pattern. This approach is advisable if your garment is to be made in a very expensive material. Alternatively, if your garment is to be made in a relatively cheap material, you can bypass the making of a toile and model your garment material directly on the stand.

As you have already been shown how to produce a pattern from the stand in Chapter 2, our first example will follow the method to be applied in making a toile and from it the finished garment. Skirts fall into four categories:

1 straight;
2 circular/flared;
3 gored;
4 draped.

We shall take each of these categories in the order listed.

If the lower part of the skirt is to be fitted to the stand, card may be attached at hip level and extended to the ankle. Alternatively, if you have a trouser stand, that would be even better.

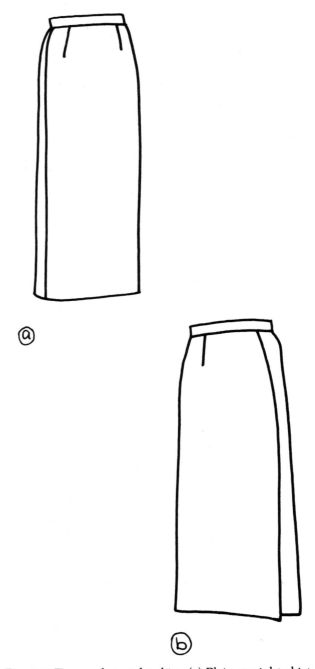

Fig. 3.1 Types of straight skirt. (a) Plain straight skirt. (b) Straight wrap-over skirt. (*c-f overleaf*).

Fig. 3.1 (*cont.*) (c) Dirndl. (d) Bell-shaped or dome. (e) Tiered. (f) All round pleated.

1. STRAIGHT SKIRTS

Skirts in this category tend to fall straight from the
hip to the desired length.

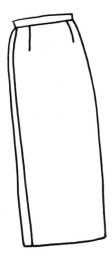

Fig. 3.2 Plain straight skirt.

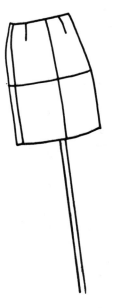

Fig. 3.3

(a) Plain straight skirt

Fig. 3.2
A plain straight skirt is one which fits the contours
of the torso from waist to hip, falling in a straight
line from the hip to whatever length is required.

Procedure

Fig. 3.3
Make a half toile or a full toile if style is fully
pleated, asymmetric, draped, or for an unbalanced
figure.

Stage 1. Adjust stand to correct height.
Stage 2. Tape your stand.
Stage 3. Select and prepare your material.
Stage 4. Place and pin material onto stand in the
following way.

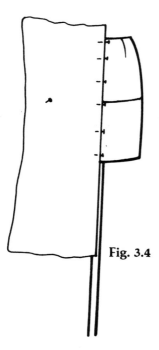

Fig. 3.4

Fig. 3.4
Pin the warp grain onto the taped centre front line of the stand down to the edge of the torso. Smooth the fabric out along the taped hipline, keeping the weft grain at right angles to the warp grain.
Pin at side seam.

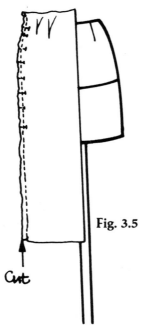

Fig. 3.5

Cut

Fig. 3.5
Pin to the taped side seam, smoothing the fabric upwards and inwards above the hipline.
Pin to side seam below hipline. Cut away surplus muslin to within 2 cm (¾″) of taped line.

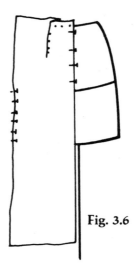

Fig. 3.6

Fig. 3.6
Smooth fabric out from the centre front along the taped waistline, pushing the excess fabric towards the taped line for the dart position.
Pin along the waistline and cut away the surplus fabric to within 2 mm (¾″).
Pin down dart line to end point.

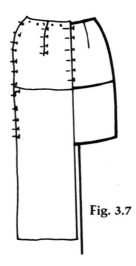

Fig. 3.7

Fig. 3.7
Smooth, pin, cut and nick along the taped waistline from the side seam, pushing the remaining excess fabric towards the dart.
Pin down other side of dart. Turn seam allowances and dart inwards. Leave on stand then model skirt back in the same manner.
Stage 5. Measure up from floor level the desired length and mark all round with pins allowing for a hem.
Stage 6. Mark in all details, e.g. stylelines, intersections, balance marks, grain lines. Remove toile from stand.

Stage 7. Press.
Stage 8. True lines and check details.
Stage 9. Check seam allowances.
Stage 10. Make up and press.
Stage 11. Place toile back on stand or live model and check for any discrepancies.

Assuming that the toile is satisfactory, you now remove it carefully from the stand. Unpick the pieces and press. These pieces now form your pattern from which you will cut your garment material. Following standard procedure, cut material and make up. As a final check, place the garment back on the stand or live model. If the finished garment is wrong, the fault must be in the making up.

Let us now go back to the point where we have fitted the made up toile onto the stand, and assume that something is wrong. Make adjustments on the stand by pinning, marking and cross marking the faults. Remove the toile from the stand, unpick the pieces, press and correct on the flat.

Using the corrected pieces as pattern pieces, cut out a full toile. Make up, leaving an opening at the back, in order that it may be pulled over the stand. Replace toile on stand and check that the previous discrepancies no longer exist. Also check that there are no new ones. If there are, repeat remedial procedure. Assuming that all faults have been rectified, simply follow the procedure described in producing the finished garment from toile pieces.

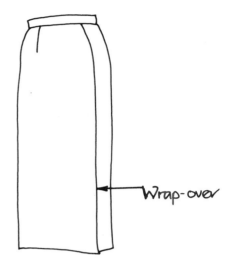

Fig. 3.8

(b) Straight wrap-over skirt

Fig. 3.8
This skirt is cut in one piece. However, if the fabric is too narrow to do this, it may be joined at one or both side seams. As it is an asymmetric design, a full pattern or toile is required.

Procedure

Follow standard preparatory stages previously described.

Tape your stand – centre front, centre back, side seam, darts, wrap-over position, waistline and hipline.
Select and prepare your material – A full toile is modelled. Allow enough material for wrap-over.
Place and pin material onto stand in the following way

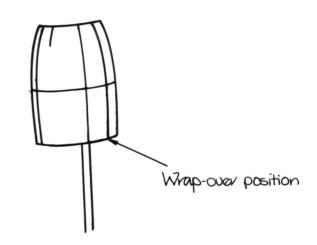

Fig. 3.9

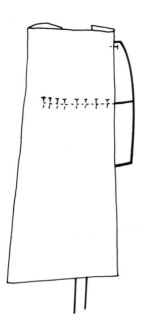

Fig. 3.10

Fig. 3.10
Along lengthwise grain, join pieces together to give required width allowing for wrap-over plus 7.5 cms (3") for facing.

Fold over the facing allowance and place the folded edge to the wrap-over position. Keep the hipline of the fabric in line with the taped hipline on the stand. Pin along the wrap-over and hip lines.

Fig. 3.11
Smooth the fabric all the way round the stand at hip level, pinning as you go. Take the fabric past the wrap-over line to a point giving required overlap and add 7.5 cms (3") for facing. It will be necessary to remove pins in order to take fabric under the wrap-over to the point of overlap, folding back the facing.

Fig. 3.12
Shape waistline as for a plain straight skirt. Any excess material left at the sides should be pushed into darts from the side seam position after the waist darts have been formed. Now follow stages 5–11 previously described.

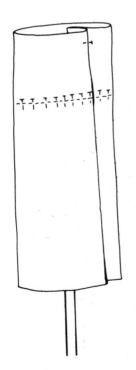

Fig. 3.11

Fig. 3.12

(c) Dirndl skirt

Fig. 3.13

A dirndl skirt is a rectangular piece of material tucked or gathered into a waistband. Sometimes, to avoid seams, or to use the border of the fabric design, it may be cut with the weft grain down the centre front. If the warp grain is to be used, then the amount of fabric gathered into the waistband is influenced by the width, type and design of fabric. You will need to experiment first with a piece of your garment material as all fabrics will tuck or gather differently.

Cut a piece of fabric approximately 30 cms × 30 cms (12" × 12"). If you are going to gather, using the largest stitch on your machine, run a row across the width and, by pulling the thread, form your gathers. Now check the resultant width measurement. For example, if the piece of fabric gathers to half its original measurement, you would need a width of material twice the waist circumference to make the skirt.

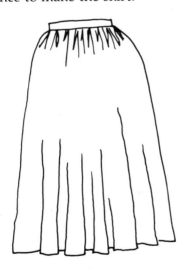

Fig. 3.13

Fig. 3.14

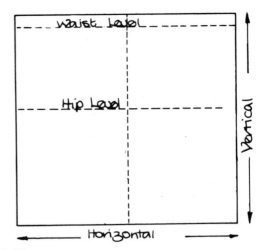

Fig. 3.15

Procedure

Fig. 3.14

Follow standard preparatory stages previously described.

Tape your stand – centre front, centre back, side seam, waistline and hipline.

Select and prepare your material – allow enough material for take up of gathers. This could be up to three times the hip measurement.

Place and pin material onto stand in the following way

Fig. 3.15

On the prepared fabric at a point some 5 cms (2") down from the horizontal edge, mark a line representing the waist level at right angles to the vertical. Following the same procedure, produce hip level line 20 cms (8") – 23 cms (9") below waist level line. These lines should align with the taped lines on your stand.

A vertical line is required to provide demarcation for alignment with the side seam position. The position of this line will be determined upon your decision as to the amount of gather you require to the front and back of the skirt.

Points to consider

Irregular figure. A large bottom, for example, may demand more gathers between side seam position and centre back than that allowed between side seam position and centre front.

Style. Placement of gathers or tucks in highlighting design points in fabric or garment.

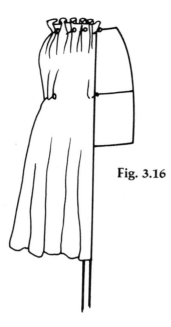

Fig. 3.16

Fig. 3.16

Pin fabric at waist and hip levels on centre front and centre back. Align vertical line with taped side seam and pin at waist and hip. To control excess material, pin above waist level.

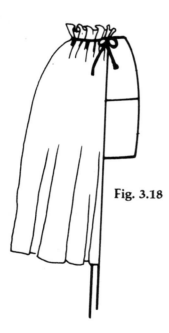

Fig. 3.18

Fig. 3.17

Tie elastic or tape tightly round the waistline and organise your gathers or tucks. Now release pin at side seam position on hipline and check hang of material.

Now follow stages 5–11 previously described.

(d) Bell-shaped or dome skirt

Fig. 3.17

Fig. 3.18

This is produced in the same way as the dirndl, but normally unpressed pleats instead of gathers are used at the waist and stiff fabrics are normally used. Softer fabrics require hooped underskirts, padding or an underskirt made of stiff fabric to hold the silhouette. Depending upon the desired effect, the fabric may be cut on the straight or bias grain.

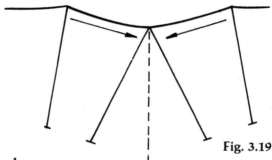

Fig. 3.19

Procedure

Follow standard preparatory stages previously described.

Follow the same procedure as for the dirndl skirt.

A very stiff material should be used for the toile. Often the tucks are placed at an angle. This is achieved by lowering the grain, in which case additional length is required – approximately 20 cms (8″). The pleats need to be marked on both sides with an arrow between the marks indicating the direction of the pleat (Fig. 3.19). Pin in tucks and hold down with a tape pulled tightly around the waist. Mark the waistline right through the folded pleats. If the fabric is pulled out from under the tape, the tucks will stand forward. Now follow stages 5 – 11 previously described.

(e) Tiered skirt

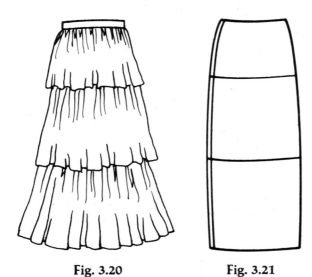

Fig. 3.20   **Fig. 3.21**

Fig. 3.20

This type of skirt is normally produced on the flat, as that is the quicker method, but modelling allows the proportion and hang to be seen more clearly – very important in this example.

The base shape of a tiered skirt can be either straight or flared. Onto the base are mounted gathered or pleated tiers. The tiers are often graduated, each tier lying under the one above it, the bottom one being the deepest.

This skirt can be produced as a variation of a flared/circular skirt (see flared/circular skirts).

Procedure

Fig. 3.21

Follow standard preparatory stages previously described.

To produce a base skirt follow the procedure described for straight skirts.

Place the finished base skirt back onto the stand.

Tape tier position on the base skirt.

Cut out tiers, gather to required amount and attach to base skirt a minimum of 2 cms (¾″) above each tier tape line.

Mark attachment lines on base skirt.

Remove tiers, tape and base skirt from stand.

True lines to hem line.

Sew tiers to attachment lines.

Now follow stages 9–11 previously described.

(f) All round pleated skirt

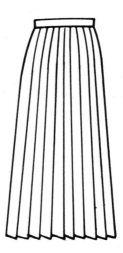

Fig. 3.22 All round pleated skirt.

Fig. 3.22

This skirt is normally produced on the flat. However, where there are figure irregularities, such as a protruding bottom, modelling facilitates regulation and adjustment of pleating when seen in three dimensions.

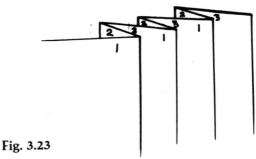

Fig. 3.23

This skirt is modelled directly in the pleated fabric. To calculate the amount of fabric required for pleating your own fabric, allow length + shrinkage allowance + hem and seam allowance for the length. As each pleat takes up an amount of fabric three times its width (Fig. 3.23), to obtain the width measurement for a knife pleat, allow three times the hip measurement + one pleat + seam allowances. (The extra pleat is used to obtain the seam allowance for the final seam.)

You can buy fabric already pleated, or have a piece of fabric professionally permanently pleated. If the latter option is chosen, vertical seams, apart from the final one, should be sewn and the fabric hemmed. The type of pleating required should be stated. Extra length needs to be added to allow for any shrinkage or unevenness which may occur with

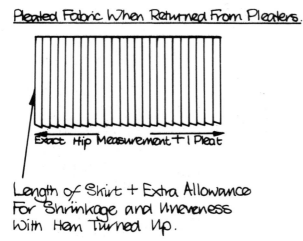

Pleated Fabric When Returned From Pleaters.

Exact Hip Measurement + 1 Pleat

Length of Skirt + Extra Allowance
For Shrinkage and Unevenness
With Hem Turned Up.

Fig. 3.24

professionally pleated fabric (Fig. 3.24). The length
will need to be corrected when the pleated fabric is
returned, by measuring up, from the hem on the
flat, the desired finished length plus waist seam
allowance.

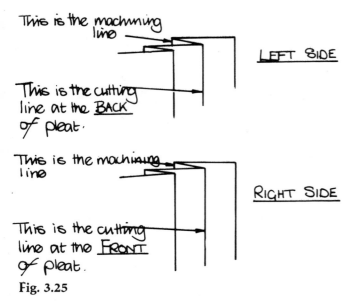

This is the machining line

LEFT SIDE

This is the cutting line at the BACK of pleat.

This is the machining line

RIGHT SIDE

This is the cutting line at the FRONT of pleat.

Fig. 3.25

Procedure

Fig. 3.25
Follow standard preparatory stages previously
described.

In order to hold the pleats in place, a tacking
thread is run round the skirt at hip level.

The extra pleat allowed for the seam allowance
should be cut as shown.

Machine this seam to within 21.5 cms (8½") of
the waist, allowing for the zip opening. Tape the
stand down the centre front, centre back, side
seams, waistline and hipline.

The whole skirt is modelled, covering the taped
lines. So that the taped lines can be found by
feeling for the pin head, sink pins into the centre of
tape.

Fig. 3.26
Place the pleated skirt on to the stand, matching
the tacked hipline of the skirt to the taped hipline
of the stand and pin. Pin down centre front from
waist to hip. Repeat at centre back.

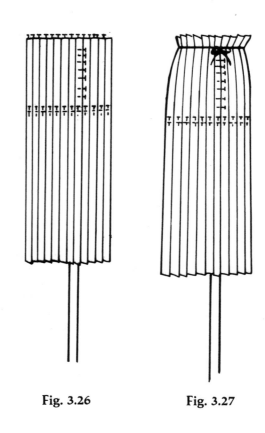

Fig. 3.26   Fig. 3.27

Fig. 3.27
Tie tape around the waist. To allow for a smaller
circumference at waist (to hip), wrap over each
pleat slightly at the waistline and pin.

A straight line taken between waistline and
established hipline will be tapered. To fit pleat to
this tapered position, pin pleat from waist to hip.
Mark the waistline.

Adjusting pleats from the hip size to the waist
size can be quite difficult if there is a large
difference. In such a case, or if the fabric is thick, or
the figure has a protruding abdomen, the pleats
are best mounted onto a yoke.

Now follow stages 6–11 previously described.

Hip yokes

Fig. 3.28

A hip yoke on a pleated skirt is an unpleated piece of fabric following the contours of the body between the waist and hips, usually without waist darts. The yoke may be extended into the lower part of the skirt (as illustrated).

Procedure

Follow standard preparatory stages previously described.

Prepare pleated fabric as before. If using a shaped yoke (as, for example, the one illustrated) then the pleated length must be from the highest point on the yoke.

Tape your stand – centre front, centre back, sides, yoke shape, waistline and hip-line.
Select and prepare your material – Allow three times width of pleat for each pleat required.
Place and pin material onto stand in the following way

Fig. 3.29

Mould fabric within the taped yoke lines, easing excess upwards and outwards towards side seams (as for the top part of a plain skirt without a waist dart) but be careful not to get the side seam too much on the bias or it will drag. Cut away surplus to within 2 cm (¾″).

Fig. 3.30

Place pleated skirt onto stand, lining up the tacked hipline of the skirt with the hipline of the stand and pin. Remove pins from lower yoke line and push surplus pleating up under the yoke line. Pin pleats to tapered line between yoke and hip. Pin top of pleat to yoke line fabric only. Remove all pins except those on yoke line. Remove skirt from stand. Just below the yoke, pin each pleat into position. This prevents pleats being distorted. Now machine across the skirt just above these pins. True.

Mark in yoke line on skirt. Place a balance mark where each pleat meets the yoke.

Cut along yoke line on pleated skirt, allowing for seams. Now follow stages 9–11 previously described.

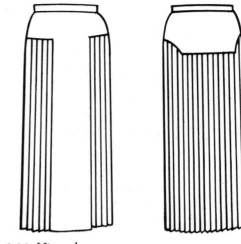

Fig. 3.28 Hip yokes.

Fig. 3.29

Fig. 3.30

Pleated skirts

Fig. 3.31–3.34
The procedure followed for pleated skirts, including yokes, applies to all pleated material irrespective of the type of pleat. The only deviation will be in calculating the width of fabric as different types of pleats demand different fullness.

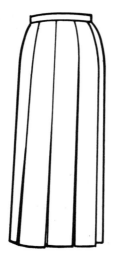

Fig. 3.31 Box pleats.

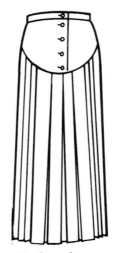

Fig. 3.32 Knife and inverted pleats.

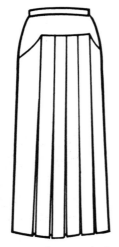

Fig. 3.33 Inverted pleats.

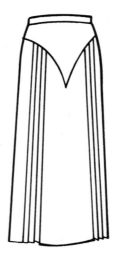

Fig. 3.34 Knife and box pleats.

2. CIRCULAR/FLARED SKIRTS

A circular/flared skirt flares out directly from the waist. The amount of fullness and placement of each flare can be controlled whilst modelling. Five types are illustrated in Figs. 3.35–3.39.

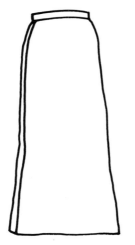

Fig. 3.35 Slightly flared skirt.

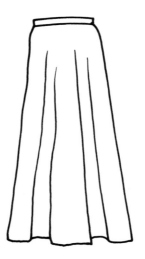

Fig. 3.36 ½ circle skirt.

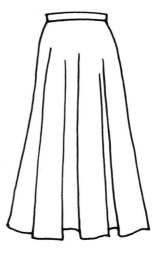

Fig. 3.37 ¾ circle skirt.

Fig. 3.38 Full circle skirt.

Fig. 3.39 Skirt with two full circles.

Variations of circular/flared skirts

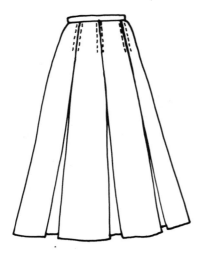

Fig. 3.40 (a) Pleated circular skirt.

(a) Pleated circular skirt (Fig. 3.40)

Pleats of any description may be placed wherever desired and are usually deeper at the hemline than the waist. They are done at the same time as the placing of the flares.

Fig. 3.42 (c) Tucked circular skirt.

(c) Tucked circular skirt (Fig. 3.42)

The tucks are machined along the fabric before modelling the skirt in the normal way.

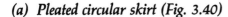

Fig. 3.41 (b) Gathered circular skirt.

(b) Gathered circular skirt (Fig. 3.41)

Gathers can be achieved by pushing in extra fullness between the flares wherever desired.

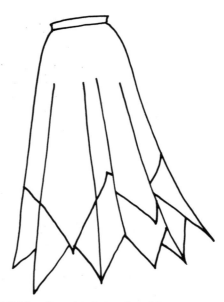

Fig. 3.43 (d) Handkerchief circular skirt.

(d) Handkerchief circular skirt (Fig. 3.43)

This can be formed in a single layer or several layers of flimsy material with pointed hems.

Fig. 3.44 (e) Gored circular skirt.

Fig. 3.45 (f) Yoked circular skirt.

(e) Gored circular skirt (Fig. 3.44)

This skirt should be modelled in the normal way then divided up on the flat mathematically into wedge-shaped sections, to any number or size of panel.

(f) Yoked circular skirt (Fig. 3.45)

The yoke is modelled first, then the skirt is modelled to the shaped yoke line, dropping the flares from the yoke instead of the waist.

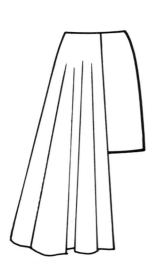

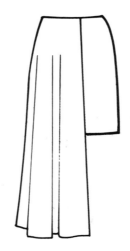

Fig. 3.47 (ii) Warp grain down princess line.

Fig. 3.46 (i) Warp grain down centre.

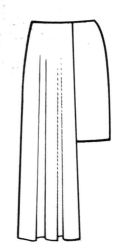

Fig. 3.48 (iii) Wrap grain down sides.

Grain

Before we proceed with modelling the circular skirt, it is important to understand the effect that grain has, firstly on the silhouette of the garment, and secondly, on the way the resultant pattern is placed on the fabric.

Figs. 3.46, 3.47 and 3.48

The silhouette of the skirt will be affected by where you place the warp grain. The warp grain on the centre front will give the fullest effect; on the side seam, the narrowest effect; and, if placed on the princess line, an effect between the two extremes.

If the centre of the skirt is placed on the warp grain, the flares will stand out, whereas if it is placed on the bias, the skirt will cling more closely to the figure. Sometimes, for economic reasons, or to avoid having to seam the material unnecessarily, the centre of the skirt is placed on the weft grain.

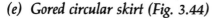

Modelling the circular/flared skirt

Procedure

Follow standard preparatory stages previously described.

Tape your stand – centre front, centre back, waistline, sideseam.

Select and prepare your material.

In selecting your material, if one width is not enough to accommodate the flare, join another length onto it along the warp grain. The join, in order of preference, would be the side seam position; if not, then the back or side front. Where the fabric has a ribbed effect, join in the same direction of the rib. The first decision to be made is where you intend placing your grain. For the first exercise, we will place the warp grain down the centre front.

(i) Warp grain down centre front and back (Fig. 3.46)

Place and pin material onto stand in the following way

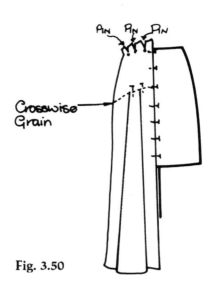

Fig. 3.50

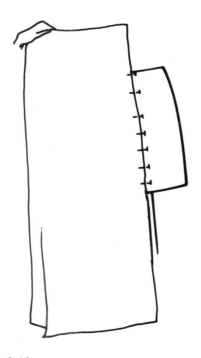

Fig. 3.49

Fig. 3.49
Holding the bulk of the fabric in your left hand, place the bottom of the fabric to the required length. Keeping the excess above the waist, pin the warp edge of the fabric at the centre front from waist to almost the end of the torso.

Fig. 3.50
Flares may be placed where you wish.

   Decide where you wish the flares to fall and how much fullness is needed. Still holding the bulk of the fabric in your left hand, lower the crosswise grain from the centre front waist. By lifting or lowering the fabric the grain will adjust fullness, allowing you to shape the flare. Each flare can be set and controlled separately. The more the grain is lowered, the greater amount of fullness will fall into a flare. Therefore if you wish to have full flares, allow plenty of excess above the waistline.

   Once you have placed a flare, pin at waist, cut away excess fabric above waistline from the centre front to the pin and nick into waist. Move along from centre front to sides, repeating the process until side seam is reached. The distance between pins at waist should be approximately 3.5 cms (1½″).

Fig. 3.51

(iii) *Warp grain down sides (Fig. 3.48)*

Follow the same procedure as for the skirt with the warp grain down the centre front. Place warp grain down side seam, pinning fabric from hipline to edge of torso along side seam tape.

Arrange the first flare in to the pinned side seam, smoothing along the hipline, pinning the flare in position. Now continue smoothing material up the side seam to waist position and pin.

At the first flare point, cut away surplus material to within 1 cm (½″) of the waist and nick. Continue in the same way to the centre front.

Pin and mark the centre front line and cut away surplus. Leave front on the stand and repeat process to form back of skirt.

Now follow stages 5–11 previously described.

Very slightly flared skirts

Slightly flared skirts require waist darts, therefore, as this is an exception to the general rules covered in Figs. 3.46, 3.47 and 3.48, we will deal with this topic separately.

Procedure

Fig. 3.52
Follow standard preparatory stages previously described.

Tape the stand – as for flared skirts, but add dart position and hipline.
Select and prepare your material as previously described
Place and pin material onto stand in the following way

Fig. 3.52

Side seam position

Fig. 3.51
Turn the fabric in on itself at the taped side seam, the seam to be perpendicular to the floor. However, for skirts with lots of fullness, allow seam to slant outwards from the hip level.

Cut away excess fabric beyond side seam position to within 2.5 cms (1″).

Crease the fabric along seam edge and fold back seam allowance to underside of fabric and repin.

Leave front skirt on stand and model the back in the same manner.

Now follow stages 5–11 previously described.

(ii) *Warp grain down princess line (Fig. 3.47)*

Follow same procedure as for skirt with grain down centre front. Place warp grain down princess line, pinning fabric from hipline to waistline. Work from princess line towards centre front and side seam gaining flares in the same way as previously described.

Finish and cut away surplus fabric to side seam.
Repeat process to form back skirt.
Now follow stages 5–11 previously described.

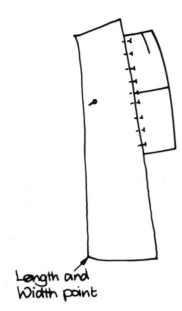

Fig. 3.53 Marking fabric length and width point.

Pin the warp grain of the fabric to the taped centre front line of the stand, allowing 5 cms (2") above the waistline for grain to be lowered.

Decide on length of skirt and width at hemline. Mark fabric length and width point (Fig. 3.53).

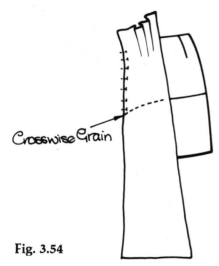

Fig. 3.54

Work at hip level first, smoothing out the fabric from the centre front, allowing the weft grain to drop enough for the determined hem width.

Pin side seams at hip level.

Mark and pin side seam in position perpendicular to the floor (Fig. 3.54).

Now follow the same procedure for fitting waist darts as in (a) plain straight skirts (see Figs. 3.5, 3.6 and 3.7).

Now follow stages 5–11 previously described.

Slightly flared skirt

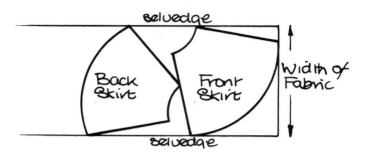

Fig. 3.55

Fig. 3.55
Centre front and back on true bias.
  Sides on any bias grain.

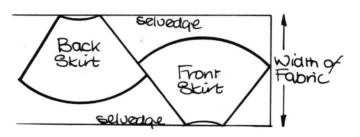

Fig. 3.56

Fig. 3.56
Centre front and back on weft grain.
  Sides on any bias grain.

¼ circular skirt

As the hemline is narrow, if the skirt fitted to waist exactly it would be too tight across the hips, therefore darts are needed at the waist. The ¼ circular skirt can be cut with the warp grain running through the centre of the skirt if you can get it into the fabric width.

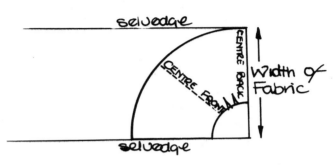

Fig. 3.57
Centre front on bias.
   Centre back on warp and weft.

Fig. 3.57

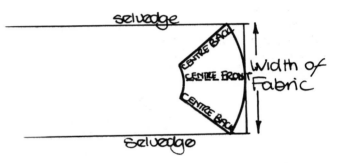

Fig. 3.58
Centre front on warp grain.
Sides on any bias.

Fig. 3.58

½ circle skirt

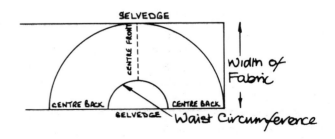

Fig. 3.59
Centre front on weft grain.
   Centre back on warp grain. (This would be reversed if skirt had a front opening and a plain back.

Fig. 3.59

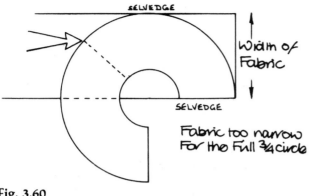

Fig. 3.60

¾ circle skirt

Fig. 3.60
If the fabric is too narrow to cut the ¾ circle skirt in one piece, the pattern should be cut in half as indicated.

You can now place the two halves of the pattern on your material in one of two ways, shown in Fig. 3.61 and Fig. 3.62.

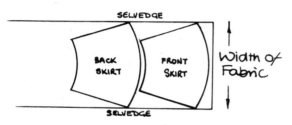

Fig. 3.61

Fig. 3.61
Centre front and back are on the warp grain and the sides are on the bias grain.

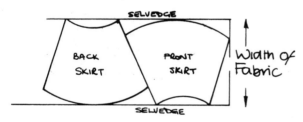

Fig. 3.62

Fig. 3.62
Centre front and back are on the weft grain and the sides are on the bias.

Full circle skirt

Fig. 3.63
Centre front and back are on the weft grain, side seams on the warp grain.

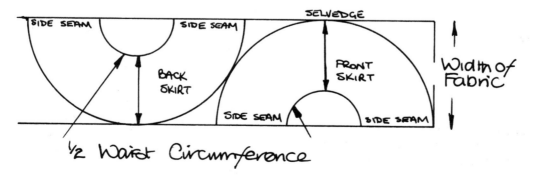

Fig. 3.63

3. GORED SKIRTS

A gore is a wedge-shaped panel which fits the waist snugly then flares out at, or below, the hip to the hemline. A great variety of skirt styles may be produced by varying the number of gores and the position of flares.

Examples are illustrated below.

When modelling, all gored skirts have straight seam lines that fall perpendicularly from the breakpoint to the floor. (Note that seam lines perpendicular to the figure will change angle at the breakpoint on the pattern.) The hem and waistlines are curved. From the breakpoint to the waist, lines are straight, apart from the side seams which are curved above hip level. The placement and the amount of flare that is added from a high or low breakpoint will influence the silhouette of the skirt. A minimum flare would be approximately 2.5 cms (1"). Whatever amount is added to a gore seam, it must be the same as that on the adjoining one. (Note – flare can differ on each side of a gore, as long as the above rule is applied.)

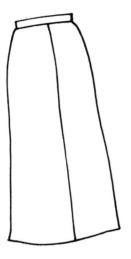

Fig. 3.64 Four gore skirt with gore seams at centre front, centre back and sides.

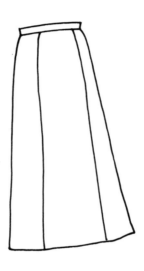

Fig. 3.65 Four gore skirt with gore seams at the princess line.

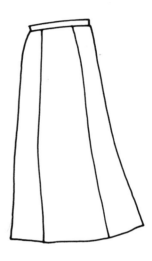

Fig. 3.66 Six gore skirt with gore seams at princess line and sides.

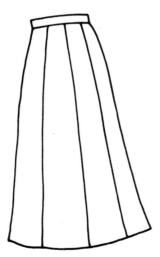

Fig. 3.67 Eight gore skirt with gore seams at centre front, centre back and sides.

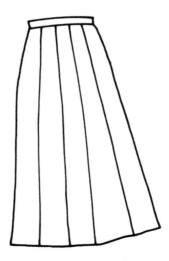

Fig. 3.68 Ten gore skirt (evenly divided).

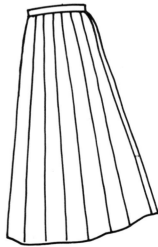

Fig. 3.69 Multiple gores (evenly divided).

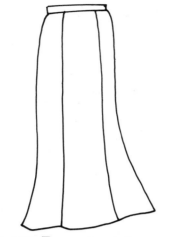

Fig. 3.70 Trumpet or tulip gores.

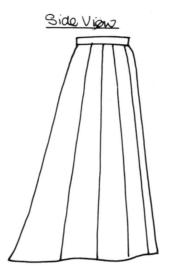

Fig. 3.71 Graduated gores.

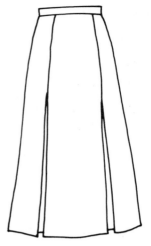

Fig. 3.72 Gores with pleats.

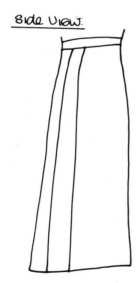

Fig. 3.73 Back gored skirt with plain front.

Fig. 3.74 Gored skirts with gathers (a) at side panel, (b) at centre panel.

Grain

A gored skirt may be cut on the warp grain, or, if a clinging effect is desired, the bias grain. Whichever is decided upon, those gores which have evenly balanced flares will have the lengthwise grain down the centre of the gore. Skirts having unbalanced flares will have the less flared edge placed first between the hip level and hemline with the vertical line of each gore parallel to the centre line on the stand. Narrow gores may have flare introduced by simply increasing the width of hem instead of lowering the crosswise grain.

Variations – gathers, tucks and pleats

Gathers, tucks or pleats should be dealt with as previously described, after the flare of the gore has been established. Pleats in gored skirts should widen towards the hem to keep the pleat from spreading and to keep the flare balanced.

For the following exercises, the skirts shall be cut on the warp grain.

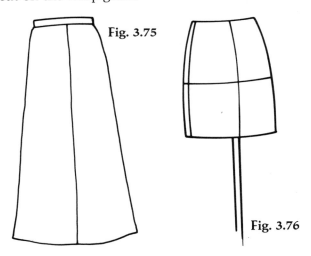

Fig. 3.75

Fig. 3.76

(a) The four gore skirt (With gore seams at centre front, centre back and sides)

Procedure

Fig. 3.75
Follow standard preparatory stages previously described.

Fig. 3.76
Tape your stand – centre front, centre back, side seam, waistline and hipline.
Select and prepare your material as previously described
Place and pin material onto stand in the following way

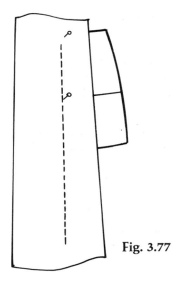

Fig. 3.77

Fig. 3.77
Hold fabric against stand with bottom at hem level and excess above waist.

Allow fabric to overlap centre front line by a minimum equal to amount of flare.

Pin at hip and waist level at the centre of the panel, the warp grain being parallel to the centre line on the stand.

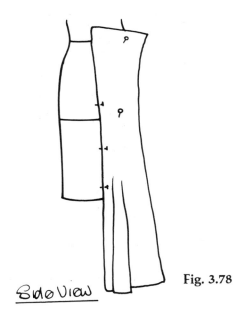

Side View   **Fig. 3.78**

Fig. 3.78
From the pinned position smooth the fabric round to the side seam and pin from just above hip level to end of torso, sloping out to form the flare.

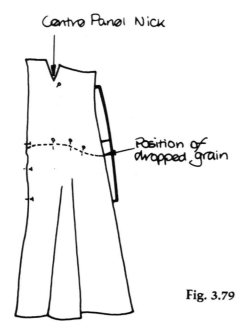

Centre Panel Nick

Position of dropped grain

Fig. 3.79

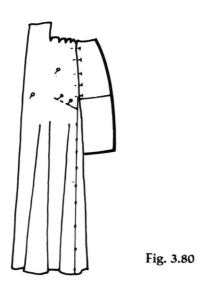

Fig. 3.80

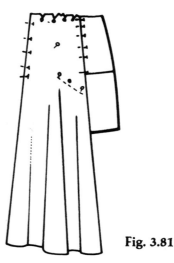

Fig. 3.81

Fig. 3.79
Nick into fabric at centre panel position above waist. First nick fabric to allow the fabric to drop at the centre front, lowering the grain for the amount of flare required at the centre of the panel.

Pin along the dropped crosswise grain at hip level to hold the flare.

Fig. 3.80
From dropped grain line and centre of panel, smooth fabric up to contours of stand and pin at centre front and waist. Pin and nick to waist. From centre front to centre panel nick waistline and cut away surplus fabric to within 1 cm (½").

Mark in centre front line with pins from hip level to hem perpendicular to the floor.

Cut away surplus from centre front line to edge of fabric.

Fig. 3.81
From centre panel to side seam smooth fabric to contours of stand from hipline to waist, pinning along side steam. Pin and nick to waist. Cut away surplus above waist to within 1 cm (½") of waistline.

Remove pins in centre of panel. Check hang of skirt.

Repeat process for half back.

Now follow stages 5–11 previously described.

For two to six gores, the same procedure is followed.

(b) The six gore skirt

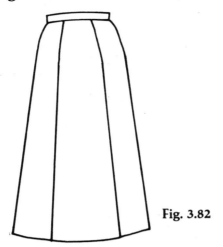

Fig. 3.82

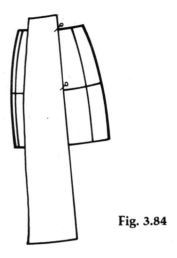

Fig. 3.84

Centre front panel

Fig. 3.82
The gore seams are at the back, front, princess line and side seam position. The six gore skirt may be adapted into a four gore skirt by removing the side seams, or into an eight gore skirt by placing a seam down the centre front and back.

Fig. 3.84
Place fabric to the stand allowing approximately 5 cms (2″) above waist level.

Pin lengthwise grain to the centre front at waist and hip.

Fig. 3.83

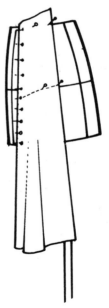

Fig. 3.85

Procedure

Follow standard preparatory stages previously described.

Fig. 3.83
Tape your stand – centre front, centre back, sideseam princess line, waistline and hipline.
Select and prepare your material as previously described
Place and pin material onto stand in the following way

Fig. 3.85
Smooth the fabric out to waist and hipline and pin on these lines approximately 6 cms (2½″) from centre to hold fabric whilst you place the flare at the bottom of the panel, by lowering the crosswise grain.

Mark width of panel at flare point and hem and crease a line between the two points. Cut to within 1 cm (½″).

Pin to stand at princess line turning under seam allowance.

Leave on stand.

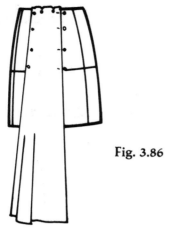

Fig. 3.86

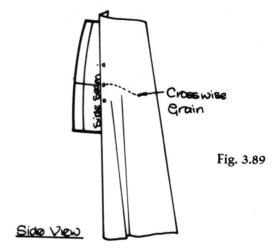

Fig. 3.89

Side View

Fig. 3.86
Smooth fabric from hipline to waist along princess line and pin.
　Cut away surplus, nick and pin waistline.

Side front panel

This can be modelled in two ways:

(a) by pinning the lengthwise grain to the form at the centre of the side panel and then modelling outwards to the front and the sides; or
(b) by commencing at the side seam working towards the princess line.

The second method is demonstrated.

Figs. 3.87 and 3.88.
Draw the desired flare on your fabric for the side seam from hip to hem. Place onto stand, matching up hip and side seam with those on stand, folding under the seam allowance. Allow fabric to fall perpendicular to the floor and pin at hip level and just above and below it.

Side panel

Fig. 3.89
Smooth out on hipline and pin fabric 6 cms (2½″) from side seam, then lower the crosswise grain to form a flare.
　Pin and lower the grain to the princess line. If you lower the grain right at the side seam the flare will fall at the side. Holding the grain as shown, it will fall at the princess line instead.

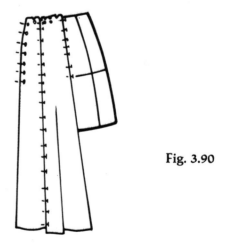

Fig. 3.90

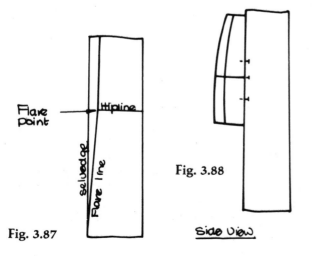

Fig. 3.87　　　　**Fig. 3.88**　　Side View

Fig. 3.90
Match the flare of the princess line with that of the centre panel. Mark width of panel at flare point and hem and crease a line between the two points. Cut to within 1 cm (½″). Push seam allowance towards sides and pin to centre panel.

Note: If seam does not fall perpendicular to the floor, it means that the crosswise grain needs to be raised or lowered and the seam remarked. By nicking into the seam allowance at the flare point more flare may be added to the gore.

(c) Multiple gores (those numbering above six)

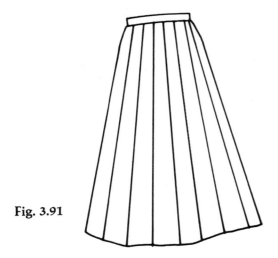

Fig. 3.91

Fig. 3.91

A multiple gored skirt is normally produced on the flat. It is possible to produce it by modelling although it is more time consuming.

Procedure

Follow the standard preparatory stages previously described.

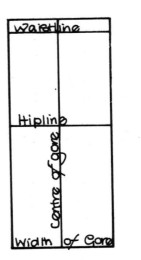

Fig. 3.93

Fig. 3.93

Select and prepare your material as previously described

Tear material into rectangles large enough to cover the length of skirt plus 5 cms (2″) for extension above waistline plus hem allowance by width allowing measurement from flare to flare at hem.

From top edge of fabric draw horizontal lines 5 cms (2″) down for waist.

From waistline measure 20 cms – 23 cms (8″–9″) and mark hipline.

Draw vertical line halfway between the two vertical edges.

Fig. 3.92

Fig. 3.92

Tape your stand – centre front, centre back, position of gore seam lines, waistline and hipline. Gores can either be of the same size, or can vary according to the effect you hope to achieve.

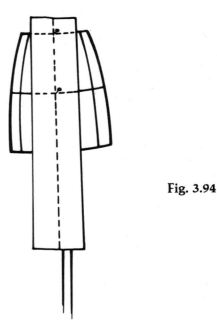

Fig. 3.94

Fig. 3.94

Place and pin material onto stand in the following way

Place the centre of fabric panel to the centre of a taped gore on the stand.

Match horizontal lines on fabric to those on the stand.

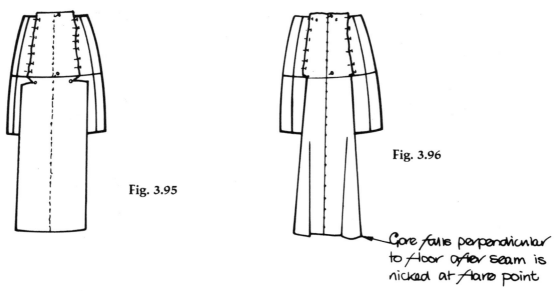

Fig. 3.95

Fig. 3.96

Gore falls perpendicular to floor after seam is nicked at flare point

Fig. 3.95
Smooth fabric out from centre to taped gore line and pin from hip to waistline and along waistline.
  Cut away surplus to within 1 cm (½").
  Nick into flare point (change of angle for flare).

Fig. 3.96
Allow the fabric to fall into a flare. Mark width of panel allowing for flare and crease a line between hem and flare point perpendicular to the floor. Cut to within 1 cm (½") of the creased line.
  Now, using this panel as a pattern, cut the rest of the gores identically.
  Now follow stages 5–11 previously described.

4. DRAPED SKIRTS

Fig. 3.97
The grain is lowered to produce flared skirts. It is raised and held at the waistline to achieve drapes. This results in the skirt clinging to the figure at the hemline.

If possible, model the skirt in the fabric itself, or a cheaper one with similar qualities, as the silhouette is affected by the characteristics of different materials. A full toile is required.

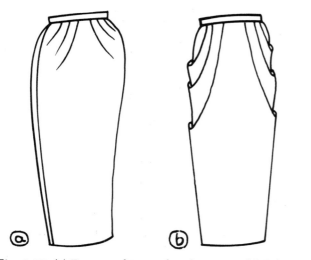
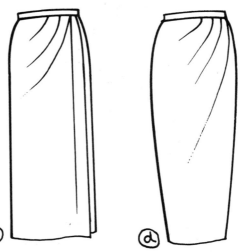

Fig. 3.97 (a) Peg top skirt with side seams. (b) Peg top skirt without side seams. (c) Draped wrap-over skirt. (d) Asymmetric draped skirt.

(a) Peg top skirt with side seams

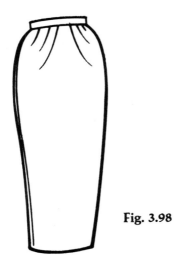

Fig. 3.98

Fig. 3.98
The peg top skirt with side seams has folds or gathers radiating out from the waistline to above the hip level.

Procedure

Follow standard preparatory procedure already described.

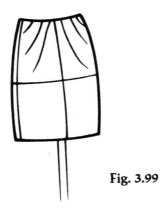

Fig. 3.99

Fig. 3.99
Tape your stand – centre front, centre back, side-seams, waistline, hipline and position of drapes.
Select and prepare your material as previously described
When estimating the amount required, allow extra for the drawing up and depth of drapes. Fold material for front skirt along its length and mark centre line.
Place and pin material onto stand in the following way

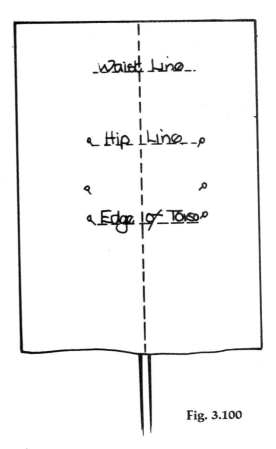

Fig. 3.100

Front skirt

Fig. 3.100
Pin the centre line onto the taped centre front line of the stand from waist to the edge of the torso. Allow enough material above waistline for drapes.

Smooth the fabric out along the taped hipline, keeping the weft grain at right angles to the warp grain. Pin at side seam down to edge of torso.

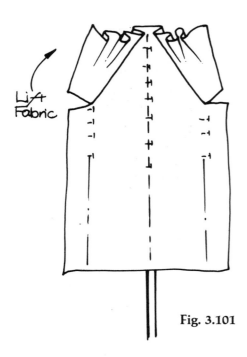

Fig. 3.101

Fig. 3.101
At the lowest taped fold line, sink a pin into stand at side seam. Nick into excess fabric to that pin. Using the pin as a pivoting point, lift the fabric and push some of the excess fabric into pleat position on taped line.

Pin this first fold.

Fig. 3.102
Repeat this procedure for as many times as there are folds.

Fig. 3.103
Place a tape round the waist to establish the waistline. If you wish the folds to stand forward, pull out the fabric from under the tape. Cut away surplus fabric to within 2 cm (¾″) at side seams and 1 cm (½″) at waist.

Leave front skirt on stand and then model back as for straight skirt or gored skirt as desired.

Now follow stages 5–11 previously described.

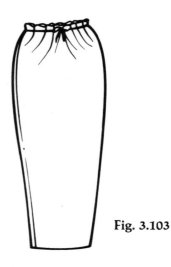

Fig. 3.103

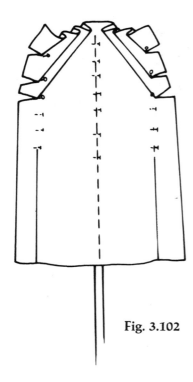

Fig. 3.102

(b) Peg top skirt without side seam

Fig. 3.104

A peg top skirt without side seams has folds or
gathers radiating out from the waist to any depth
on the skirt at the sides. The front and back are
modelled simultaneously.

Procedure

Follow standard preparatory stages previously
described.

Fig. 3.105

Tape your stand – centre front, centre back, side seam
position, waistline, hipline and position of drapes.
Select and prepare your material as previously described

Note: This style is very extravagant with material. It
would be advantageous for your first attempt at
making the toile to use some cheap material,
allowing you to assess the quantity required for
this style.
Place and pin material onto stand in the following way

Fig. 3.106

Pin edge of material down centre back allowing
approximately 7.5 cms (3") beyond the waistline.

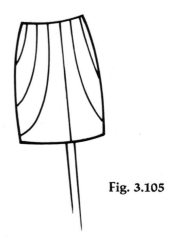

Fig. 3.105

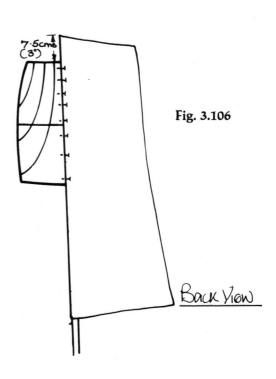

Fig. 3.106

Back View

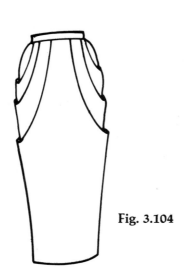

Fig. 3.104

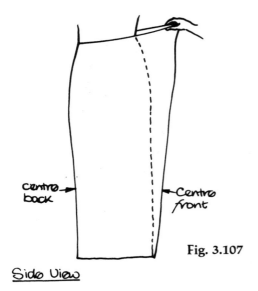

Fig. 3.107

Side View

Fig. 3.107
Wrap the fabric round the torso, holding the centre front away from the waistline and raising it so that the fabric lies close at the hem. This will cause the centre front to lie on a bias grain. The more the grain is lifted, the more bias the centre front will become and the more fullness allowed in the folds. If a centre front seam is to be avoided, the centre front must be on the true bias as anything outside a true bias would result in one half of the skirt falling on a different grain to the other and so causing the skirt to hang incorrectly.

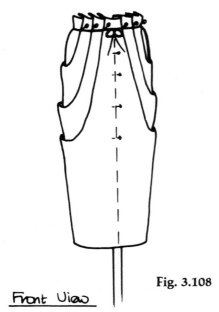

Front View

Fig. 3.108

Fig. 3.108
From waist to edge of torso, pin down centre front line.
Position folds at front and back to design on each

side, pinning as you go. Tie a tape around the waist. Adjust folds if desired, by pulling the fullness forward from under the tape.

Mark in taped waistline, position and direction of folds and hemline.

Cut away surplus round waist to within 1 cm (½").

Now follow stages 5–11 previously described.

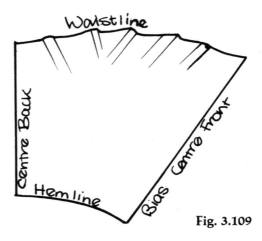

Fig. 3.109

Fig. 3.109
The final pattern will have the centre back on the warp grain and the centre front on a bias grain. The hemline will be curved. (If the warp grain is down the centre front, then the back will be on the bias.)

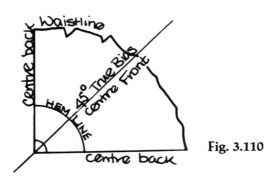

Fig. 3.110

Fig. 3.110
If centre front lines are on the true bias (i.e. 45°) then one centre back seam will be on the warp grain and one on the weft grain. Because of this, the chosen fabric should have similar properties on the warp and weft grain in order for the skirt to hang correctly.

(c) Draped wrap-over

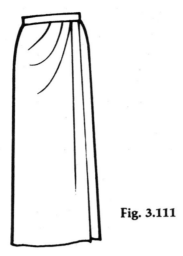

Fig. 3.111

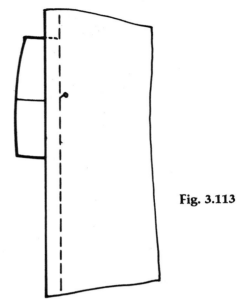

Fig. 3.113

Fig. 3.111
In this style, if possible, avoid draping below hip level, as there is a tendency either to pull too tightly across the legs for comfort, or not to pull tightly enough, causing displacement of the side seam.

Procedure

Follow standard preparatory stages previously described.

Fig. 3.113
Select and prepare your material as previously described
Allow extra material for the drawing up of folds and approximately 7.5 cms (3″) above the waist level and 12.5 cms (5″) beyond the sides.
Place and pin material onto stand in the following way
Beginning at the right side seam, pin the fabric to the stand at hip level, allowing 12.5 cms (5″) approximately beyond the side seam for the slanting of the seam.

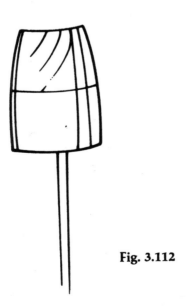

Fig. 3.112

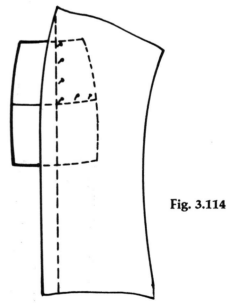

Fig. 3.114

Fig. 3.112
Tape your stand – side seams, waist, hipline, centre back, drapes and wrap-over position.

Fig. 3.114
Smooth the fabric along the weft grain at hip level and pin approximately 10 cm (4″) in. Then work upwards towards the waist on side seam, pinning and pushing the surplus fabric inwards.

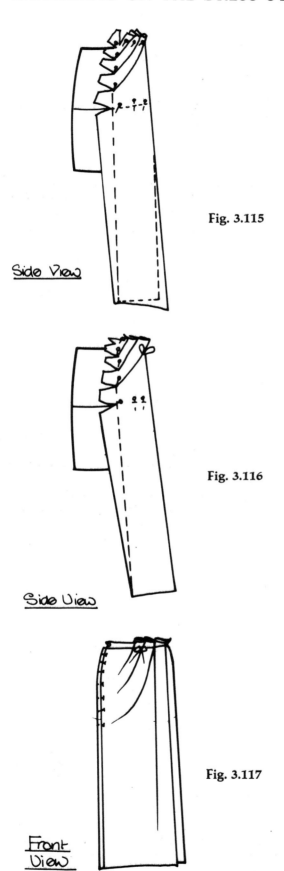

Side View

Fig. 3.115

Side View

Fig. 3.116

Front View

Fig. 3.117

Fig. 3.115
Nick and pin into side where the fabric is stretched, to allow the placing of the folds to cling to the stand. Along fold position, working from the side to the centre, place the fold by raising the grain at the bottom in the direction indicated by the taped stand. The fold disappears at the side seam. (Observe how the side seam becomes more bias the more the fabric is pulled up.)

Follow the same procedure for each fold (depending on the angle of the fold, it is not always necessary to raise the grain).

The grain can be kept level, or even lowered slightly towards the centre, this giving a very deep fold as indicated in Fig. 3.116.

Should the grain be lowered, then it will slant outwards producing a wider hem.

Fig. 3.117
Place a tape round the waist over the folds to establish the waistline. Mark in the centre front and position and direction of folds. Cut off excess at waist to within 1 cm (½") and pin along waistline.

Mark in the centre front line, side seams, waistline and position and direction of folds.

Model left side of skirt front and back skirt as for a straight skirt. Check the balance of the side seam with right side of skirt.

Note: The resultant shape (Fig. 3.118) will be irregular. Leave curves, angles and edges as they are.

Now follow stages 5–11 previously described.

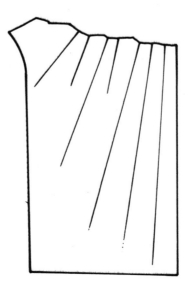

Fig. 3.118

(d) Asymmetric draped skirt

Fig. 3.119

Fig. 3.119
This skirt is modelled in the same way as the draped wrap-over skirt.

Procedure

Follow standard preparatory stages previously described. Follow the stages for producing the draped wrap-over skirt, but here take the last waist fold over to the opposite side seam intersection.

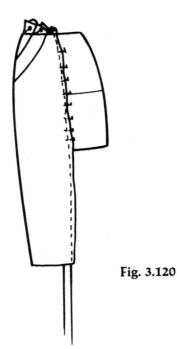

Fig. 3.120

Fig. 3.120
Pin left side of skirt onto taped side seam position and cut away surplus at sides to within 2 cms (¾″). (Check angle of side seam with right side of skirt to balance.)

Leave front on stand and model back skirt.

Now follow stages 5–11 previously described.

CHAPTER 4
BODICES

A BASIC BODICE BLOCK

The block is produced as a record of shape and size. Onto the block the designer will build style.

In order to fit a flat piece of material to the contours of the body it is necessary to allow enough material for extremities, while suppressing the surplus fabric away from the apex. On a basic block this suppression is normally in the form of darts. The greatest amount of suppression is needed where there is the greatest curve, i.e. directly below the bust. A basic block normally has two darts in order to provide good fitting and a rounded effect over the bust points. These two darts are normally either at the waist and shoulder or the waist and underarm. These are the combinations that give the best fitting for a basic block. However, darts can be placed anywhere round the bust, but must always point towards the bust point.

The stand is taped for the position of the darts and the surplus fabric pushed towards and into those dart positions.

It is also possible to push all the surplus fullness into one dart. This will give a more pointed effect over the bust. If a more rounded effect is desired, then the surplus can be suppressed into three darts. Alternatively, all the suppression can be in the form of tucks, drapes, folds, gathers and seams, etc.

Darts should not vanish at the bust point itself, but finish approximately 2.5 cm (1″) away.

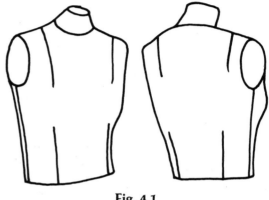

Fig. 4.1

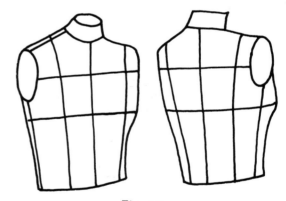

Fig. 4.2

Modelling a basic bodice block

Fig. 4.1

Procedure

Follow standard preparatory procedure previously described.

Fig. 4.2

Tape your stand – centre front, centre back, neckline, side seams, waistline, shoulders, armhole, bustline, chestline, backline, and seam demarcation lines from shoulder to waist (for dart positions).
Select and prepare your material as previously described
Place and pin material onto stand in the following way

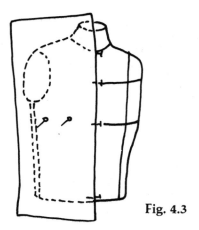

Fig. 4.3

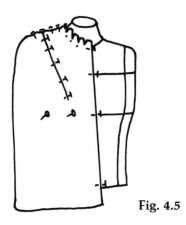

Fig. 4.5

Front

Fig. 4.3
Place the warp grain of the muslin along the middle of the taped centre front line, allowing enough material for the height of the shoulders, depth of the torso and width of half a front bodice.

Pin down the centre front at the neck, chest, bust and waist. Keeping the weft grain at right angles to the warp grain, smooth the fabric out towards the bust point and pin on apex, then to side seam, and pin.

Fig. 4.5
Push excess muslin up from above the bustline to shoulder dart and out from neckline towards the shoulder dart. Pin onto taped shoulder dart to within 2.5 cm (1") of bust point.

Push fullness of dart under creased line away from armhole.

Cut away surplus muslin beyond shoulder line to within 2 cms (¾").

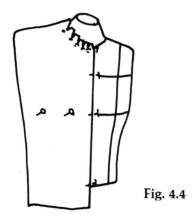

Fig. 4.4

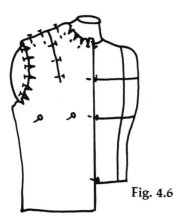

Fig. 4.6

Fig. 4.4
From the centre neck, smooth the muslin away round the neck and towards the shoulder, pinning onto the taped line and cutting away the surplus muslin to within 1 cm (½") of the neck.

Nick into the neckline so that the fabric will lie smoothly round the taped line.

Fig. 4.6
Smoothing the fabric out and down from shoulder, pin fabric onto taped shoulder and armhole, cutting away surplus fabric to within 1 cm (½") and nicking into the curve.

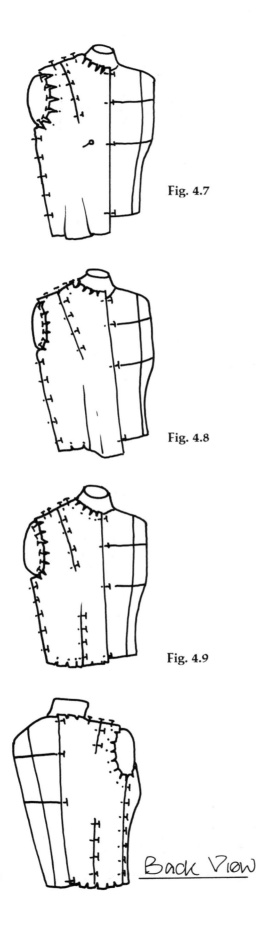

Fig. 4.7

Fig. 4.8

Fig. 4.9

Fig. 4.10

Back View

Fig. 4.7
Pin muslin down the taped side seam, smoothing the surplus fabric towards the waist dart.

Cut away fabric to within 2 cms (¾") of side seam line.

Remove temporary pin at underarm level.

Fig. 4.8
Pin the muslin along the taped waistline, cutting away the surplus fabric and nicking into the seam. Push the muslin into the waist dart position and sink pins into the taped line.

Remove temporary bust pin.

Fig. 4.9
Now move the centre front waist, pinning, smoothing and nicking the fabric outwards away from the centre front towards the waist dart.

Remove temporary pins from the taped dart position.

Push the fullness of the dart towards the centre and crease along the dart line.

Pin down the taped waist dart from 2.5 cms (1") below bust point.

Turn in seam allowances around neck edge and sink in a row of pins to hold the edge. Leave front bodice on stand, but move shoulder and side seam pins away from seam position by approximately 2.5 cms (1").

Back bodice

Fig. 4.10
The back bodice is modelled in the same way as the front, the fullness being over the shoulder blades instead of the bust point. The length of the shoulder dart is approximately 7.5 cms (3") and the waist dart 18 cms (7").

Now follow stages 6–11 previously described in Chapter 3.

You have now produced a half toile for a basic bodice. Using the same procedure, many different permutations can be achieved by pushing the excess material into different dart positions. A number of examples are illustrated on the following pages.

Note: Darts or seam position can be changed into gathers, tucks or pleats. These can be used in place of the darts previously illustrated.

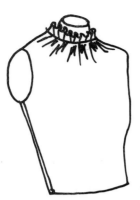

Fig. 4.11 Gathers.

Gathers

Fig. 4.11
Using the largest machine stitch, the thread may be pulled to bring the gathering into the desired length. Alternatively, the fabric can be pushed into gathers with the edge of your shears, and machined over, using a normal machine stitch. It can be held in position by an ungathered panel.

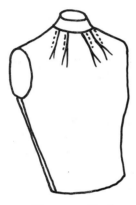

Fig. 4.12 Tucks.

Tucks

Fig. 4.12
Tucks are the same shape as the darts, but instead of continuing to the point are machined only part of the way down either inside or outside the tuck. They should be marked along both sides and at the end of each tuck to indicate both the shape and length. The direction of the tuck should be indicated by an arrow inside the tuck.

Fig. 4.13 Pleats.

Pleats

Fig. 4.13
Pleats can be folded over then stitched or not stitched, pressed or unpressed.
Mark both sides of the pleat at seam allowance.

POSSIBLE DART POSITIONS, KEEPING THE WAIST DART IN ITS NORMAL POSITION

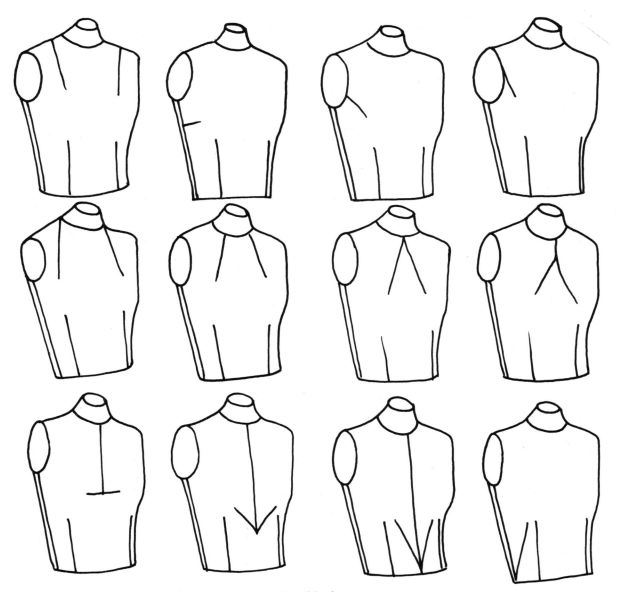

Fig. 4.14 Possible dart positions.

Fig. 4.14
Keeping the *waist* dart in its normal position, move
the excess round the outer edges to produce a
different design. The darts shown above may be
run into each other over the bust point to form
seam lines which can be straight or curved as
illustrated in Fig. 4.15.

Making darts into seam lines

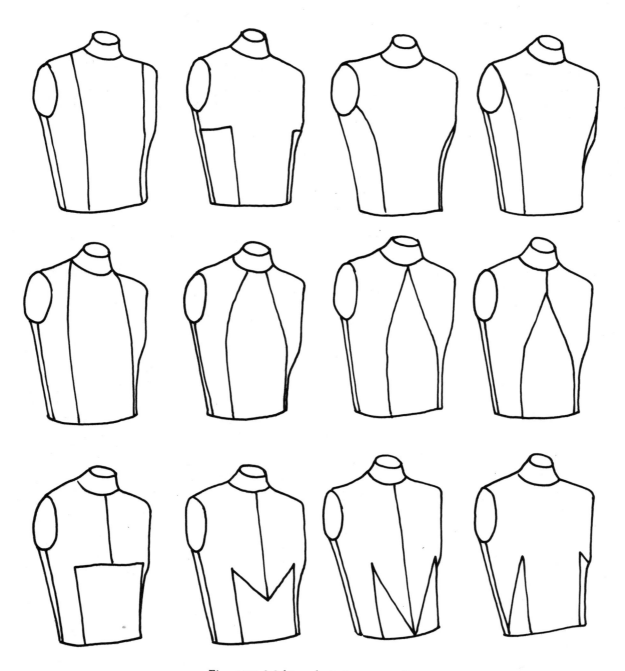

Fig. 4.15 Making darts into seam lines.

POSSIBLE DART POSITIONS, KEEPING THE SHOULDER DART IN ITS NORMAL POSITION

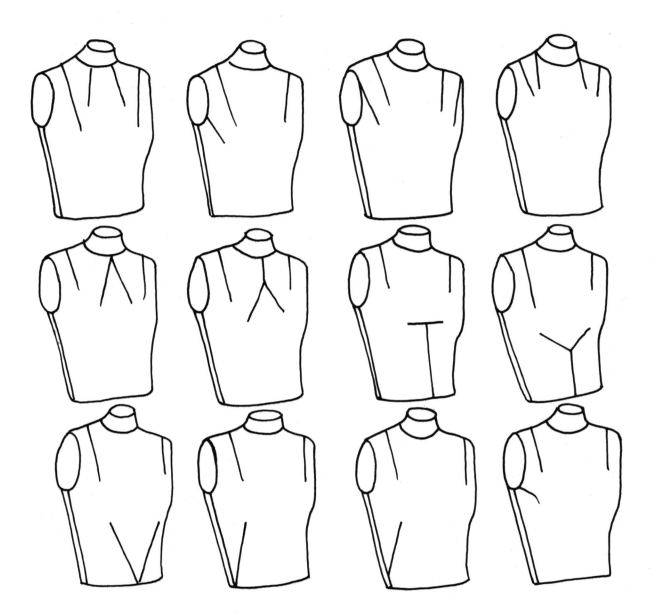

Fig. 4.16 Possible dart positions, keeping the shoulder dart in its normal position.

Fig. 4.16
Keeping the *shoulder* dart in its normal position, move the excess round the outer edges to produce different designs. The darts shown above may be run into each other over the bust point to form seam lines as illustrated in Fig. 4.17.

Making darts into seam lines

Fig. 4.17 Making these darts into seam lines.

POSSIBLE DART POSITIONS, KEEPING THE BUST DART IN ITS NORMAL POSITION

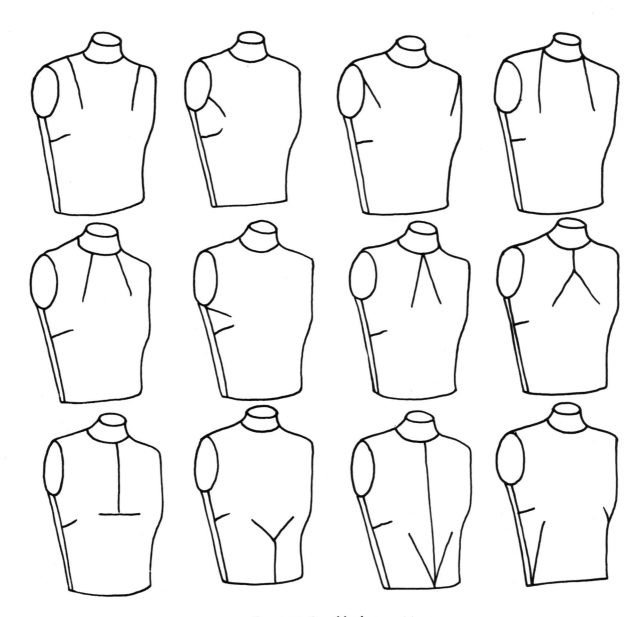

Fig. 4.18 Possible dart positions.

Fig. 4.18
Keeping the *bust* dart in its normal position, move
the excess round the outer edges to produce a
different design. The darts shown above may be
run into each other over the bust point to form
seam lines as illustrated in Fig. 4.19.

Making darts into seam lines

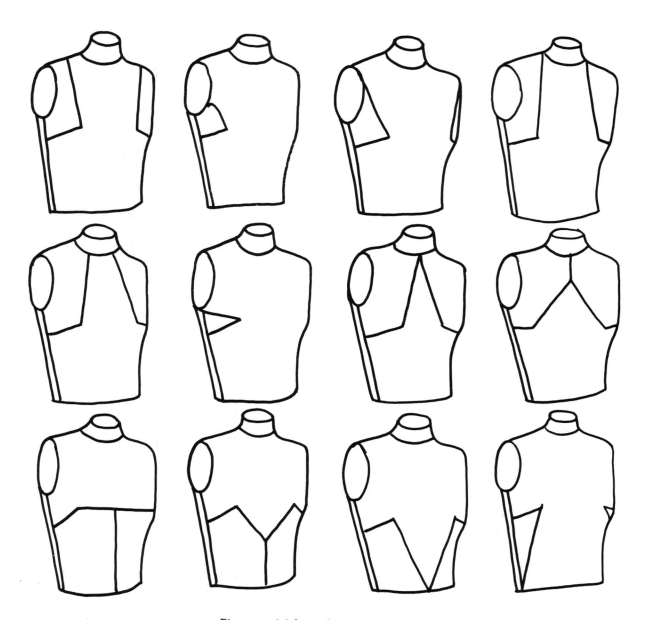

Fig. 4.19 Making darts into seam lines.

OTHER POSSIBLE DART POSITIONS

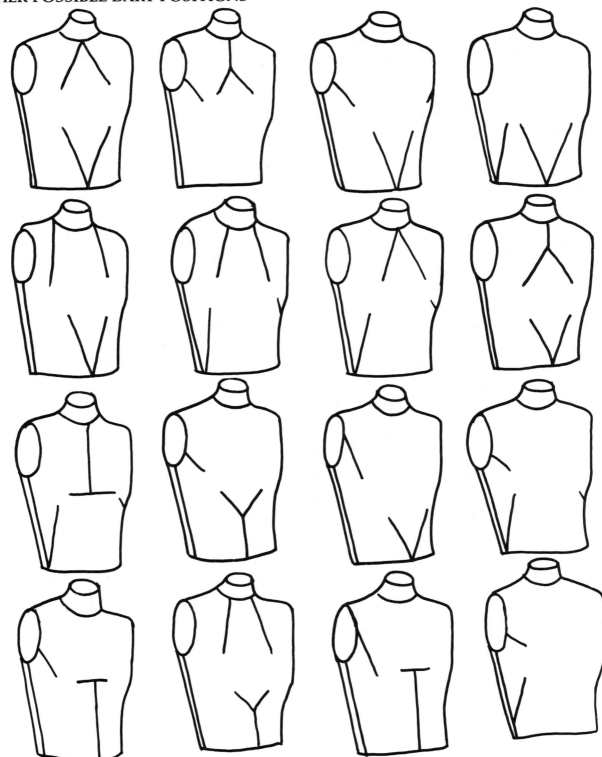

Fig. 4.20 Other possible dart positions.

Fig. 4.20
Any dart may be kept in its normal position whilst the excess is moved around to produce different designs. These are a few examples. Again the darts can be run into each other to form seam lines or divided into extra darts or converted into tucks as illustrated in Fig. 4.21

Making these darts into seams

Fig. 4.21 Making these darts into seam lines.

EXTRA DARTS OR TUCKS

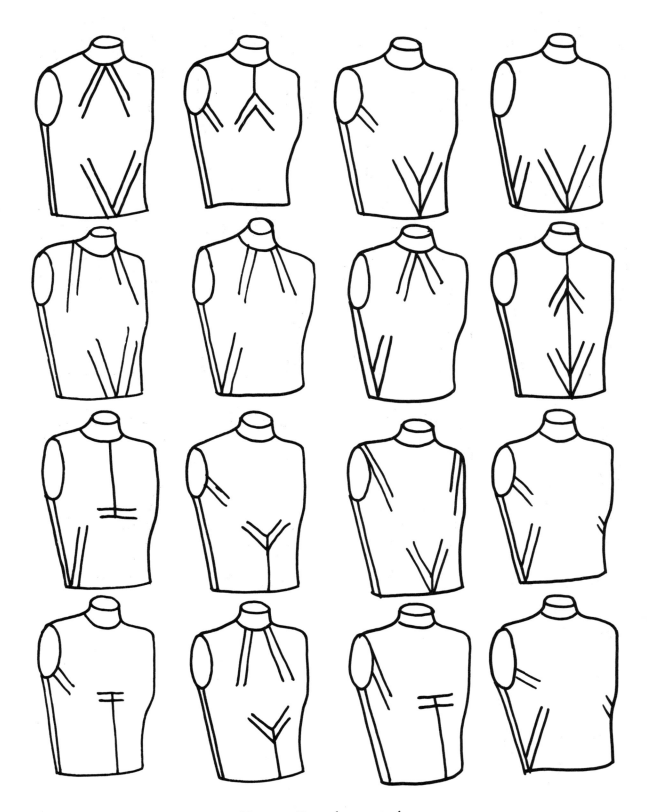

Fig. 4.22 Extra darts or tucks.

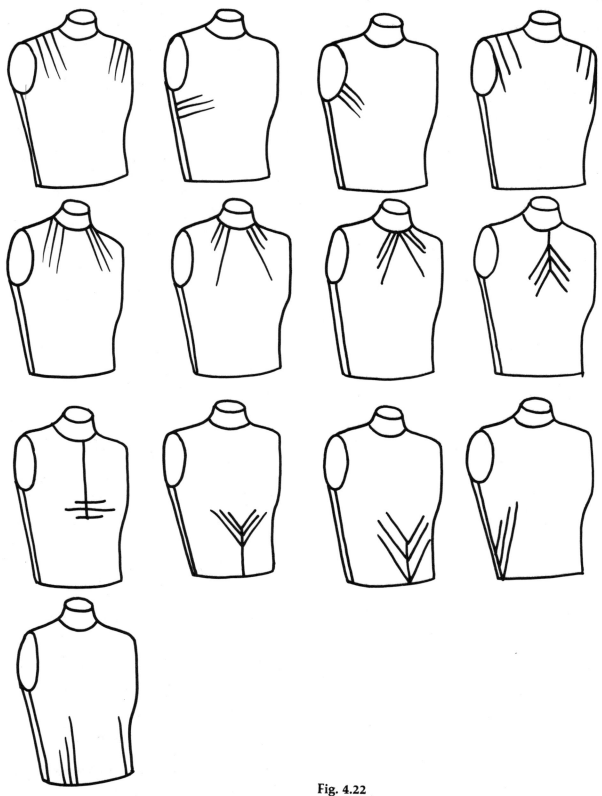

Fig. 4.22 Extra darts or tucks (*cont.*)

Fig. 4.22
Excess fabric may be smoothed into extra dart
positions instead of just two.

FULLNESS FROM INTERNAL SEAMS

If a seam does not lie over the bust point, extra fullness must be taken into the seam.

Style A

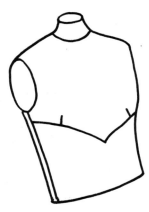

Fig. 4.23 Fullness from internal seams – Style A.

Procedure

Follow standard preparatory stages previously described.

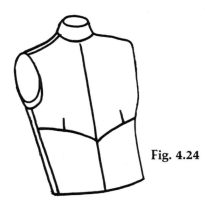

Fig. 4.24

Fig. 4.24
Tape your stand – centre front, centre back, side seam, shoulders, armholes, waistline, neckline, style line and dart position.
Select and prepare your material as previously described
Place and pin material onto stand in the following way

Midriff panel

The midriff panel is the fitted shaped section between the under bust and waistline. It is modelled as for a fitted bodice without waist darts.

Fig. 4.25

Fig. 4.25
Place lengthwise edge to centre front and pin onto taped centre front line.
    Put in temporary pin under bust point.

Fig. 4.26

Fig. 4.26
Smooth muslin out from centre front towards side seams. Cut away fabric at waistline to within 1 cm (½″).
    Pin and nick approximately every 1 cm (½″).

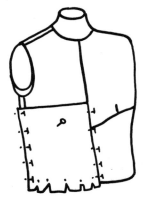

Fig. 4.27

Fig. 4.27
Smooth fabric upwards from waistline and out from centre to lie close to the body without drag lines. Pin and cut away surplus at side seams to within 2 cms (¾″).

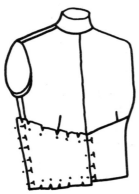

Fig. 4.28

Fig. 4.28
Remove temporary pin under bust. Smooth fabric to taped style line. Cut away surplus muslin to within 1 cm (½″) and pin.
    Leave on stand.

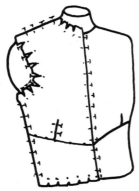

Fig. 4.29

Top bodice panel

Fig. 4.29
Model as for bodice with waist dart only.
    Smooth all excess fabric round towards under the bust dart.
    Fold dart in with its fullness pushed under towards the centre front. Allow the seam allowance to lie downwards on the style line.
    Now follow states 6–11 as previously described in Chapter 3.

Style B

Fig. 4.30 Fullness from internal seams – Style B.

Procedure

Follow standard preparatory stages previously described.

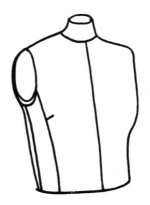

Fig. 4.31

Fig. 4.31
Tape your stand – centre front, centre back, side seam, shoulders, armholes, waistline, bustline, neckline, style line and dart position.
Select and prepare your material as previously described
Place and pin material onto stand in the following way

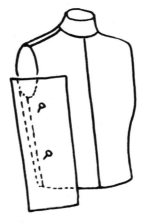

Fig. 4.32

Side panel

Fig. 4.32
Place centre of material to the centre of the panel with the lengthwise grain parallel to the centre front and pin at bust and midriff level in the centre of the panel.

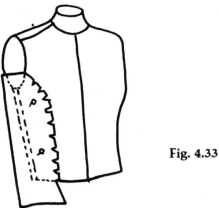

Fig. 4.33
Smooth fabric round to taped style line and pin, cutting away surplus to within 1 cm (½″) and nicking where necessary on curved lines.

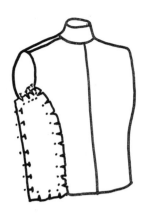

Fig. 4.36

Fig. 4.36
Cut away surplus fabric around armhole to within 1 cm (½″) and pin. Remove bust and midriff pins. Reposition style line pins back approximately 2.5 cms (1″) from taped line.

[Now follow stages 6–11 as previously described in Chapter 3.]

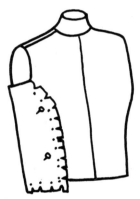

Fig. 4.34

Fig. 4.34
Smooth away from style line and pin waistline, cutting away surplus to within 1 cm (½″) nicking if necessary.

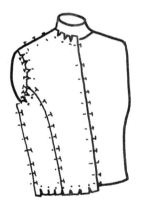

Fig. 4.37

Centre bodice

Fig. 4.37
Model as for bodice with bust dart only, pushing all surplus fabric into bust dart.

When style line is reached, cut away surplus fabric to within 2 cms (¾″). Turn seam allowance towards sides on style line then repin over seam line. Now follow stages 6–11 previously described in Chapter 3.

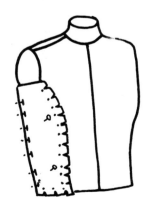

Fig. 4.35

Fig. 4.35
Smooth along up the side seams towards the armhole. Cut away surplus to within 2 cms (¾″) and pin.

Examples of various styles which can be obtained by using fullness from internal seams

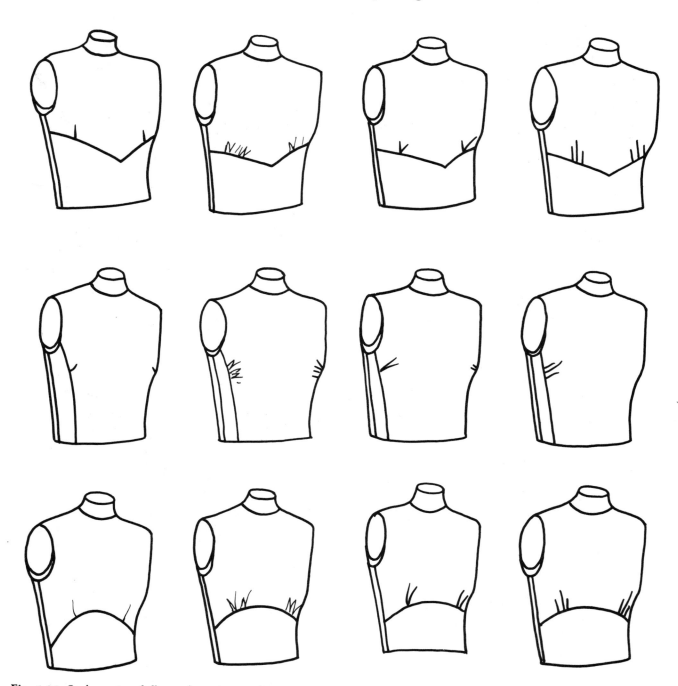

Fig. 4.38 Styles using fullness from internal seams.

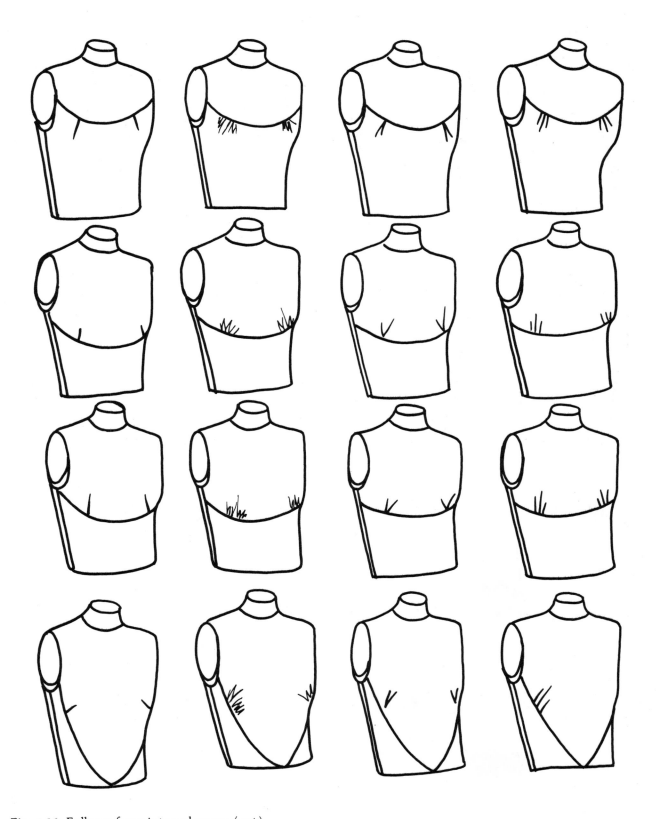

Fig. 4.38 Fullness from internal seams (*cont.*)

YOKES

A yoke is the area between the shoulder and bust. It is modelled as for a bodice without shoulder darts. It may be plain or shaped (see yokes on skirts).

Full yoke

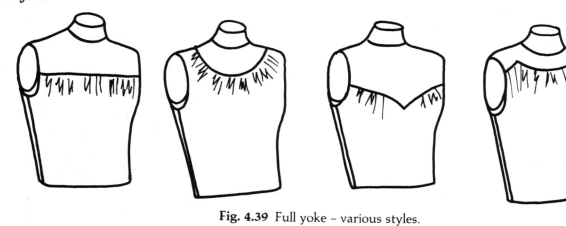

Fig. 4.39 Full yoke – various styles.

Half yoke

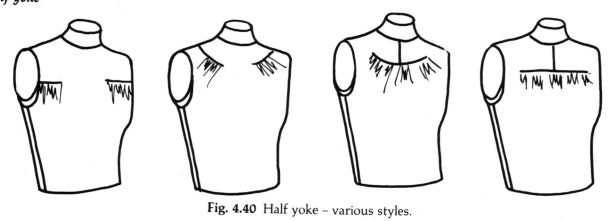

Fig. 4.40 Half yoke – various styles.

Gathered yoke

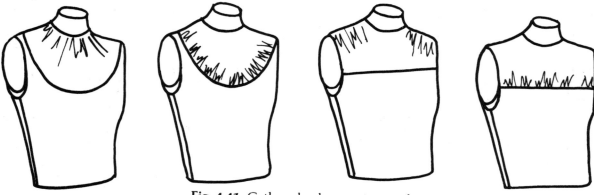

Fig. 4.41 Gathered yoke – various styles.

Full yoke style – style (d)

Fig. 4.42 Full yoke style.

Fig. 4.42
(*Note:* All full yokes follow the same procedure.)

Procedure

Follow standard preparatory stages previously described.

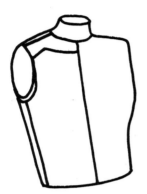

Fig. 4.43

Fig. 4.43
Tape your stand – centre front, centre back, side seam, shoulders, armhole, waistline, neckline, yokeline.
Select and prepare your material as previously described
Place and pin material onto stand in the following way

Yoke

Fig. 4.44

Fig. 4.44
Model yoke between taped lines following the method used for basic bodice block without shoulder dart. Turn seam allowance under. Pin and leave on stand.

Bodice

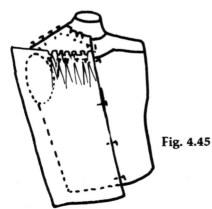

Fig. 4.45

Fig. 4.45
Pin lengthwise edge of fabric to centre line of stand. Model as for basic bodice with shoulder dart, so that all the surplus ease is pushed into area above the bust along yoke line.

If a waist dart is required, less ease will be available for gathers at the yoke, and the fabric will be modelled as for a basic bodice with shoulder and waist dart. The fullness is best centred over the bust rather than evenly distributed across the whole of the front.

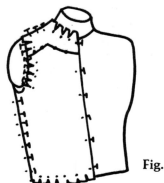

Fig. 4.46

Joining yoke and bodice

Fig. 4.46

Join the yoke to the lower bodice by taking the yoke edge over the bodice and pinning perpendicularly to the edge.

Now follow stages 6–11 previously described in Chapter 3.

Half yoke – style (c)

Fig. 4.47

Procedure

Follow standard preparatory stages previously described.

Tape your stand – centre front, centre back, side seam, shoulders, armhole, waistline, neckline, yokeline.

Select and prepare your material as previously described

Place and pin material onto stand in the following way

Fig. 4.47 Gathered yoke.

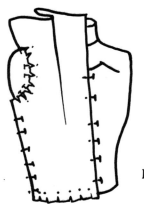

Fig. 4.48

Fig. 4.48

Pin lengthwise grain to centre line of stand.

Model as for a basic block with shoulder dart.

Push a pin into stand where yoke ends.

Fig. 4.49

Fig. 4.49

Cut along the yoke style line to pin from centre line. Keeping upper section out of the way, arrange your tucks or gathers and pin along style line.

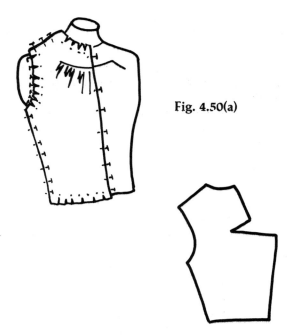

Fig. 4.50(a)

Fig. 4.50(a)
Smooth upper section around shoulders to the neck following the taped outer edges. Pin onto taped yoke line, folding over the seam allowance onto gathered section. The seam allowance will taper off at the end of the gathering.

Fig. 4.50(b) The approximate resultant shape.

Cut away surplus on outer edges to within 1 cm (½″). Figure 4.50(b) shows the approximate resultant shape.

Now follow stages 6–11 previously described in Chapter 3.

Fig. 4.51 Gathered yoke.

Gathered yoke – style (b)

Fig. 4.51

Procedure

Follow standard preparatory stages previously described.

Fig. 4.52

Fig. 4.52
Tape your stand – centre front, centre back, side seams, shoulders, armhole, waistline, neckline, yokeline.
Select and prepare your material
Place and pin material onto stand in the following way

Yoke

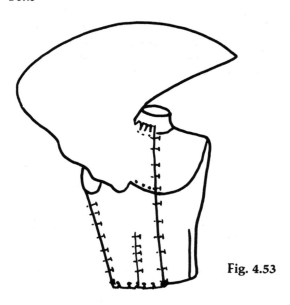

Fig. 4.53

Fig. 4.53
Pin warp grain to centre front line, allowing plenty of fabric above the yoke.

Note: The curved yokes with gathers will form a circular shape when finished. Allow enough fabric for this.

Lower the grain onto the yoke style line, arranging gathers. Cut away surplus, nick and pin.

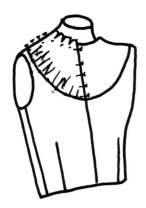

Fig. 4.54

Fig. 4.54
Smooth, nick and pin the neckline simultaneously until shoulder line is reached.

Cut away surplus to within 1 cm (½″).

Bodice

Fig. 4.55(a)
Model as for basic block with darts where desired, e.g. bodice illustrated has waist dart only. Figure 4.55(b) shows the approximate resultant shape.

Now follow stages 6–11 previously described in Chapter 3.

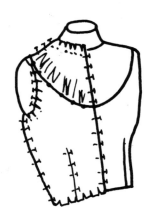

Fig. 4.55(a)

Fig. 4.55(b) The approximate resultant shape.

FLANGES

A flange is a dart, tuck or pleat used decoratively at the end of the shoulder. It may extend into just the back or front of the bodice or both. To hold it in position, it is usually top-stitched. Some examples of flanges are given below.

(a) Diminishing shoulder to apex flange

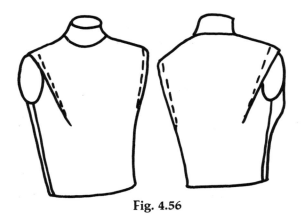

Fig. 4.56

Fig. 4.56
Model as for a bodice with shoulder dart placed at end of shoulder.

(b) Diminishing shoulder to waist flange

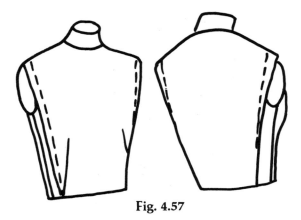

Fig. 4.57

Fig. 4.57
   Model as for basic block with waist dart only.
   For flange, mark in position and extend width of fabric to accommodate the flange at the end of the shoulder. Model out to shoulder edge and end of dart.

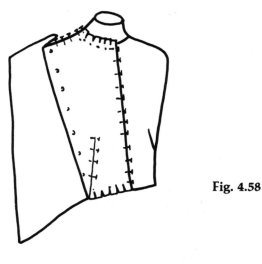

Fig. 4.58

Fig. 4.58
Fold over flange to desired depth at shoulder diminishing to waist dart and pin down following the creased line (approximately 2.5 cms (1") away from edge at top to nothing at waist).

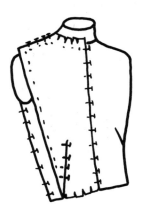

Fig. 4.59

Fig. 4.59
To complete the bodice, smooth fabric round waist, side seam and armhole, in the same way as for a basic block.
   Now follow stages 6–11 previously described in Chapter 3.

(c) Flange lengthwise to waist

Fig. 4.60

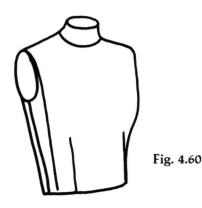

Fig. 4.60

Procedure

Follow standard preparatory stages previously described.

Tape your stand – centre front, centre back, side seam, shoulders, armhole, waistline, neckline, dart position, flange position.

Select and prepare your material as previously described

Place and pin material onto stand in the following way

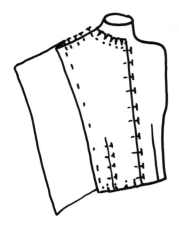

Fig. 4.62

Fig. 4.62
Fold over flange to desired depth parallel from shoulder edge (or beyond) down to waist.

Pin approximately 2.5 cms (1″) away from the creased line.

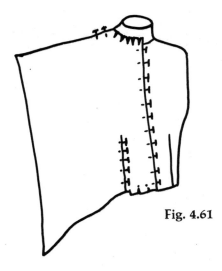

Fig. 4.61

Fig. 4.61
Model as for basic block with waist dart only, but extend width of fabric to accommodate a flange from shoulder to waist.

Model out to shoulder edge and end of dart.

Fig. 4.63

Fig. 4.63
Smooth fabric round to complete bodice round waist, side seam and armhole in the same way as for a basic block. Now follow stages 6–11 previously described in Chapter 3.

ASYMMETRIC DRAPES

Asymmetric drapes need a full toile; as can be seen, one side is different from the other. All draped styles are best modelled in the fabric itself, or a cheaper one possessing the same qualities.

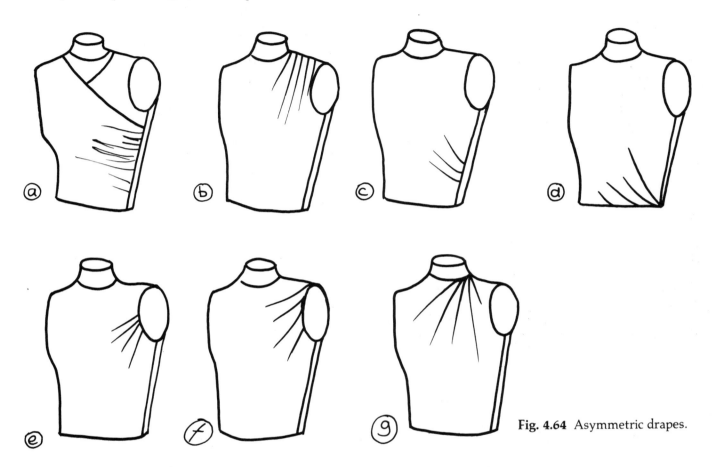

Fig. 4.64 Asymmetric drapes.

Fig. 4.64
Illustrated in Fig. 4.64 are examples of asymmetrically draped bodices. The same basic procedure is followed in modelling each style. We will use style (a) for our exercise.

Procedure

Follow standard preparatory stages previously described.

Fig. 4.65
Tape your stand – centre front, centre back, neckline, side seams, waistline, shoulders, armhole and drape positions.
Select and prepare your material as previously described
Place and pin material onto stand in the following way

Fig. 4.65

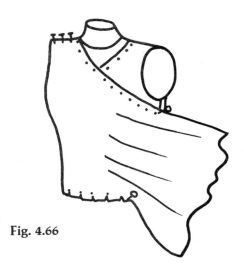

Fig. 4.66

UNDERARM COWL

Fig. 4.68

Fig. 4.66
Model as for a block with one dart position with all the dart fullness smoothed into the area of the drape.

Leave plenty of excess fabric beyond the seam edges with which to experiment.

Fig. 4.68
The underarm cowl usually has no underarm seam, but is cut in one piece with the half front and half back modelled simultaneously. To keep bulk to a minimum under the arm, thin fabric should be employed.

Procedure

Follow standard preparatory stages previously described.

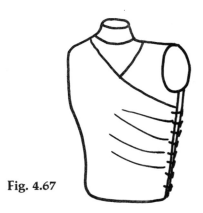

Fig. 4.67

Fig. 4.69

Fig. 4.67
Smooth drape into seam and hold with pins.

Cut away surplus to within 2 cms (¾″) seam allowance.

Mark direction and position of drapes from start to side seam position.

If it is a wrap-over style, the under bodice is modelled as for a basic block with dart.

Now follow stages 6–11 previously described in Chapter 3.

Fig. 4.69
Tape your stand – centre front, centre back, neckline, side seam (this should be centralised, i.e. the same distance from the centre front to the sides as the centre back to the sides), armhole position, waistline, shoulders, cowl positions.
Select and prepare your material as previously described

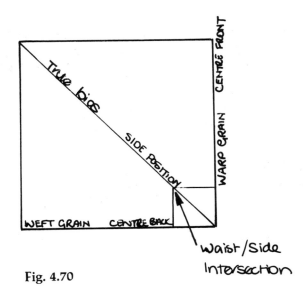

Fig. 4.70

Fig. 4.70

Cut a square of material approximately 76 cms × 76 cms (30" × 30"). Mark in a line along the true bias. On the stand at waist level, measure the distance from the centre front to the side seam and add 7.6 cms (3"). Now, on your fabric, draw in the waistline as illustrated.

Draw in line 1 cm (½") below waistline for seam allowance. The area of fabric between this line and the fabric edge is cut away.

Nick into seam allowance at side/waist intersection.

Place and pin material onto stand in the following way

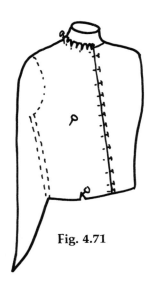

Fig. 4.71

Fig. 4.71

Place the nicked intersection point to the taped side seam at the waist and pin remainder of fabric temporarily to back and front of stand.

Smooth away from side seam along waist to princess line at front and pin.

Smooth up to bust point and pin, keeping the lengthwise grain parallel to the centre front.

Continue up to shoulder in the same way and pin.

Pin along centre front line and cut away surplus.

Smooth, pin and nick fabric around neckline from centre front to shoulder.

Repeat for back bodice.

Join shoulder seam and pin.

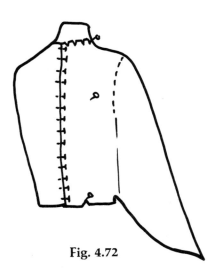

Fig. 4.72

Fig. 4.72

Holding the excess fabric out from the shoulder with the left hand, decide on the cowl depth position. For the first cowl make the depth of fold less at the shoulder than at the underarm.

This fold is brought up, shaping it towards the shoulder. If folds do not meet at the shoulder, make sure the front and back are at the same level.

This procedure is repeated for the number of cowls required.

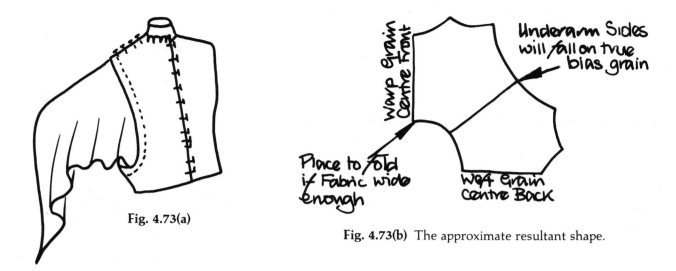

Fig. 4.73(a)

Fig. 4.73(b) The approximate resultant shape.

Fig. 4.73(a)

Cut away surplus fabric once the number of cowls are obtained, but leave an extension of fabric for a deep facing approximately 7.5 cms (3″).

Separate the front and back shoulders, keeping the cowl drapes pinned. Fold back the cowl facing and nick. Repin shoulders.

The remainder of the bodice is then modelled as desired. Figure 4.73(b) shows the approximate resultant shape.

Now follow stages 6–11 previously described in Chapter 3.

WAISTLINE AND ARMHOLE VARIATIONS

Waistlines

Procedure

Tape stand to style, taking suppression to fashion waist instead of normal waistline and proceed in the normal way to model the garment.

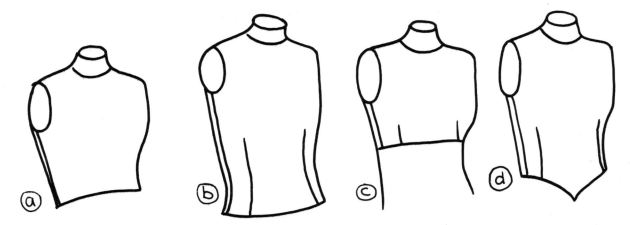

Fig. 4.74 Styles of waistline. (a) Shortened. (b) Lowered. (c) Empire. (d) Pointed.

Armholes

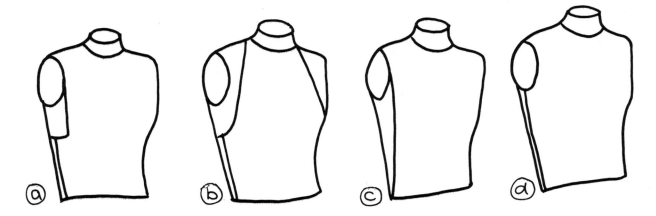

Fig. 4.75 Style of armholes. (a) Square. (b) Cut-away. (c) Pointed. (d) Raised.

Procedure

Model bodice as desired. Place stay tape over the bodice on the stand to the design required. Sleeveless designs usually need the ease reduced but this depends upon the fashion and fabric used. To reduce the ease, if the stand has collapsible shoulders, push them in before modelling. If the stand does not have collapsible shoulders, this ease may be reduced on the flat.

ALL-IN-ONE BASIC SHAPES

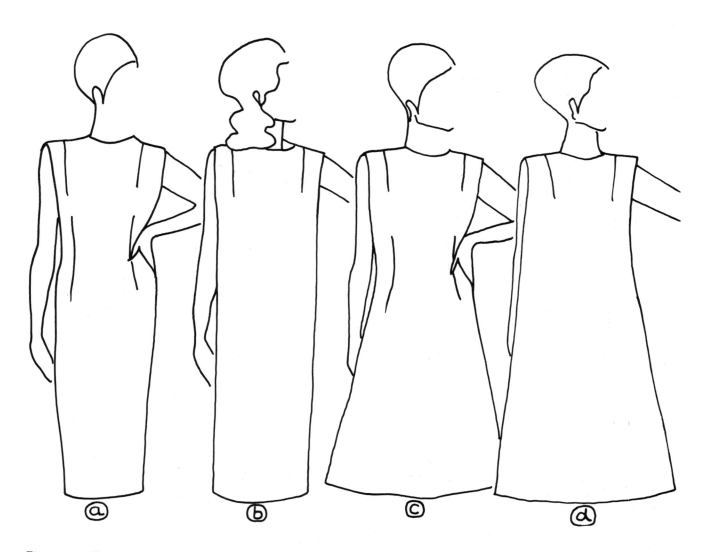

Fig. 4.76 All-in-one basic shapes. (a) Fitted straight
shift. (b) Loose straight shift. (c) 'A' line. (d)
Tent.

Fig. 4.76
By combining the bodice and skirt an all-in-one
shaped garment is achieved. The basic shape is a
straight shift which can be either fitted or left loose
at the waist. A flared shape can also be achieved
with either a fitted waist, giving an 'A' line shape,
or left loose giving a tent shape.

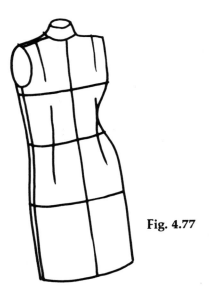

Fig. 4.77

(a) Fitted straight shift

Procedure

Follow standard preparatory stages previously described.
Adjust stand to correct height

Fig. 4.77
Tape your stand – centre front, centre back, neck, sides, waistline, shoulders, armhole, bustline, dart positions, hipline.
Select and prepare your material as previously described

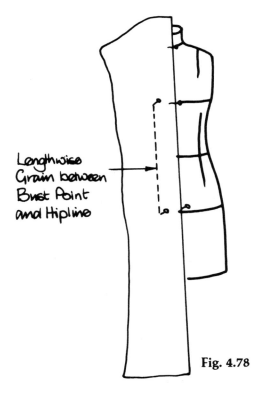

Lengthwise Grain between Bust Point and Hipline

Fig. 4.78

Fig. 4.78
Tear material to estimated length, allowing for skirt length and shoulder. Place temporary pin lengthwise edge to centre front on stand, allowing enough material to reach the neck and shoulder intersection. Ensure that enough material exists below hipline; mark for skirt length. Smooth the fabric out to bust point from centre front; mark in bust point and pin. Continue smoothing down the centre front. Mark where centre front parallel grain from the bust point meets the hipline. Pin and mark. Now remove muslin from stand.

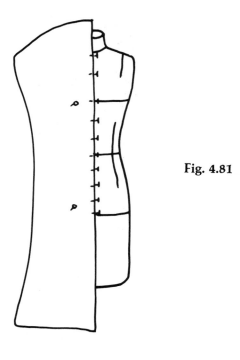

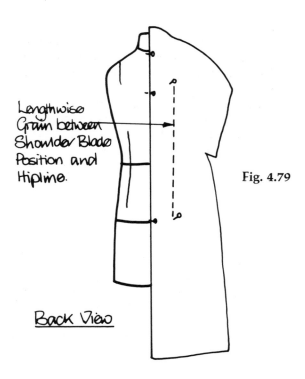

Lengthwise Grain between Shoulder Blade Position and Hipline.

Fig. 4.79

Back View

Fig. 4.81

Fig. 4.79
Follow the same procedure for the back. Ensure that the length of fabric below hip mark corresponds to that of the front. The grain line between shoulder blades at hip level to be parallel to centre back line. Mark shoulder blade position.

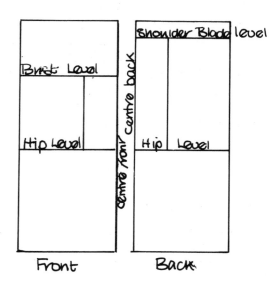

Front   Back

Bust Level

Shoulder Blade level

Hip Level   Hip Level

centre front   centre back

Fig. 4.80

Fig. 4.80
Now remove muslin from stand.

With both pieces of fabric on the flat, draw crosswise grain lines through marked points at hip level at front and back bust and shoulder blade levels. Draw in the lengthwise grain between bust point and hip level and shoulder blade position and hip level.

Place and pin material onto stand in the following way

Fig. 4.81
Place the lengthwise edge of the fabric to the stand, matching up the bust and hip level marks on the material with the taped bustline and hipline on the stand. Pin down centre front from neck to hip level. Pin at bust point, keeping lengthwise grain at hip level.

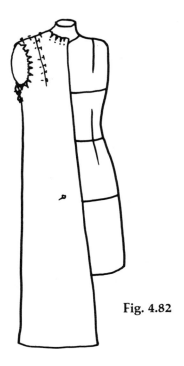

Fig. 4.82

Fig. 4.82
Model the toile above the bust level as for a bodice.

Front toile

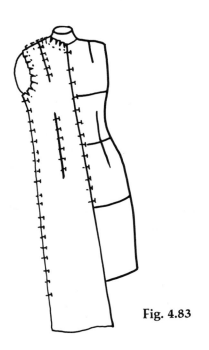

Fig. 4.83

Fig. 4.83
Pin down side seam position, and if desired, ease the fabric a little at bust and hip level.

Cut away fabric to within 2 cms (¾″) of seam line.

Smooth fabric out from centre front towards taped waist dart position and pin to dart taped line.

Repeat the procedure from the side seam.

Whilst back is modelled, reposition pins on front toile further away from the outer seam edges.

Back toile

Follow the same procedure as for front, following the body contours at the side seam at waist level, avoiding any diagonal pull on toile. Cut away surplus around the shaping to within 2 cms (¾″) of seam line.

Now follow stages 5–11 previously described in Chapter 3.

The loose straight shift (see Fig. 4.76(b))

This is modelled in the same way without any fitting around the waist.

The 'A' line (see Fig. 4.76(c))

Follow the same procedure as modelling for the fitted shift but add flare at the side seam (maximum flare 7.5 cms (3″) at knee level).

Additional flare in the front or back may be added by using the excess taken up in any dart placed above bust level, by smoothing the excess out and down into the lower part of the garment.

The tent (see Fig. 4.76(d))

Model in the same way as for 'A' line but with a straight line taken from the underarm point to the hem. The flare at the side seam may be extended to 12.5 cms (5″) at knee level.

Allow extra width of fabric for this style.

Fig. 4.84 Princess line styles. (a) Slim fitting princess line with straight flare. (b) Fully flared fitted princess line. (c) Tent shaped princess line.

THE PRINCESS LINE

We previously used the princess line for modelling the stand cover/basic block. To achieve flare in the skirt, the same procedure is used as for gored skirts. The garment is made up of full length gores (panels) which can extend either from the shoulder or from any outer edge above bust level.

Fig. 4.84
The princess line is produced in three basic shapes. For our next exercise, we shall model a princess line tent style (style 3).

Tent-shaped princess line

Procedure

Follow standard preparatory stages previously described.

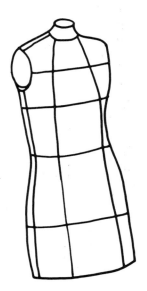

Fig. 4.85

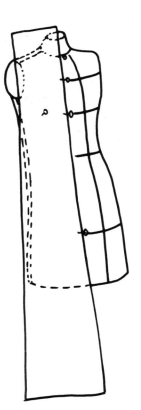

Fig. 4.86

Fig. 4.85

Tape your stand – centre front, centre back, neck, side seams, waistline, shoulders, armholes, princess line, hipline, bustline, chestline, back line.
Select and prepare your material as previously described
Allow enough width of fabric in each gore to achieve flare required.
Place and pin material onto stand in the following way

Centre front panel

Fig. 4.86

Place the lengthwise grain along the middle of the taped centre front line. Pin at the neck, chest, bust and hips. Keeping the crosswise grain at right angles, smooth the fabric out towards the bust point and pin onto apex.

Fig. 4.87

From the centre front neck, smooth the fabric away around the neck towards the princess style line, pin, cutting away the surplus material to within 1 cm (½") of the neck, nicking and pinning.

Fill in with pins down centre front between neck, chest and bust at approximately 5 cms (2"). Slash down princess line, allowing 2 cms (¾") off taped line for seam. Now pin from neck to bust. Mark details.

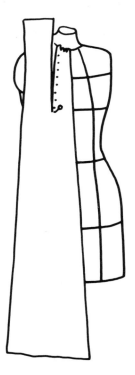

Fig. 4.87

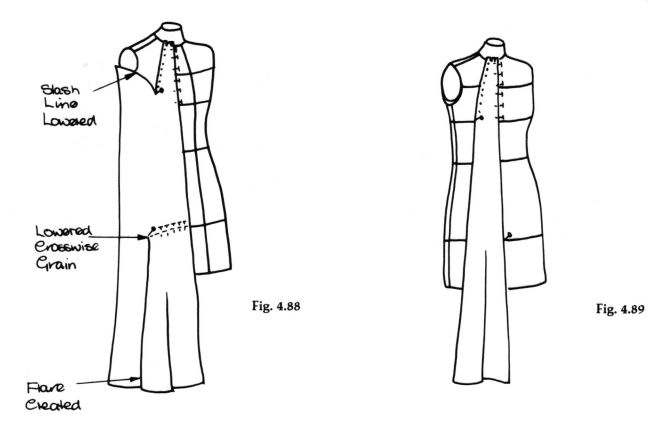

Slash
Line
Lowered

Lowered
Crosswise
Grain

Fig. 4.88

Flare
Created

Fig. 4.89

Fig. 4.88
Lower the crosswise grain by dropping the slash
line. This will create flare at the hemline. Decide on
the amount required, then pin along the dropped
crosswise grain at hip level to hold the flare.

Fig. 4.89
Mark width of flared panel at hem and mark upper
section.
  Remove from stand.
  On the flat draw a straight line between bust
mark and hem width panel mark.
  Cut away surplus to within 2 cms (¾″).
  Pin back on stand as illustrated.
  Leave on stand.

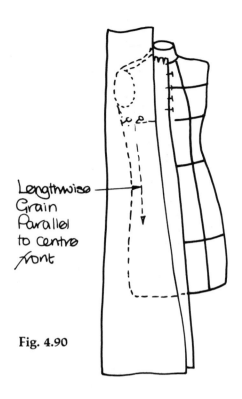

Lengthwise Grain Parallel to Centre front

Fig. 4.90

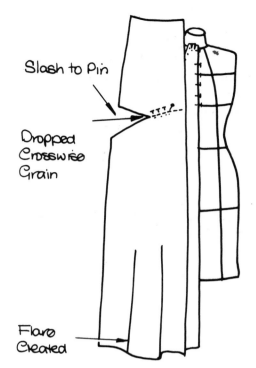

Slash to Pin

Dropped Crosswise Grain

Flare Created

Fig. 4.91

Side front panel

Fig. 4.90
Place centre of material to centre of the panel with the lengthwise grain parallel to the centre front. Pin at bust level.

Smooth fabric out towards side seam at bust level and pin at side seam.

Fig. 4.91
Slash into fabric from side to side seam and pin. Using the pin as a pivoting point, allow the fabric to drop at the sides.

Pin from side seam along bust line to apex.

Fig. 4.92
Now model top part of side panel as for a fitted bodice, smoothing all excess fabric into princess style line at neck down to bust level. Cut surplus away down princess line to within 2 cm (3/4") and tuck seam allowance under seam. Slash from side to bust pin.

Using pin as a pivoting point, allow the fabric to drop at princess line until the amount of flare matches that on centre front panel. Pivoting on side seam, slash to pin. Balance flare. Mark width of flare at hem. Mark in all details.

Remove from stand.

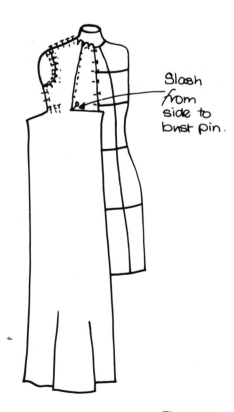

Slash from side to bust pin.

Fig. 4.92

Fig. 4.93

Fig. 4.94 (a) The empire line. (b) The dropped line.

Fig. 4.93

On the flat, draw a straight line between hem width mark and the point of bust level at side seam. Cut away surplus to within 2 cms (¾").

Pin back on stand.

Check that the princess seam line falls perpendicular to the floor.

Turn under seams to adjoining panels.

Leave on stand and model back in same way.

Now follow stages 5–11 previously described in Chapter 3.

The fully-flared fitted princess line (Fig. 3.84, style (2)) is modelled in the same way, but waistline shaping is necessary.

Extra darts may be necessary for a nipped in waist.

Other shapes include the empire line, and the dropped waist (Fig. 4.94).

In general terms, to achieve these shapes, simply follow modelling procedures for bodices and skirts joining panels where style demands.

PEPLUM

A peplum is a lengthwise addition to a bodice ending around hip level to form a jacket. It may be straight, flared, circular, gathered, pleated, draped or tucked, with a straight or shaped hemline.

It is modelled in the same way as a skirt.

Fig. 4.95 Various styles of peplum.

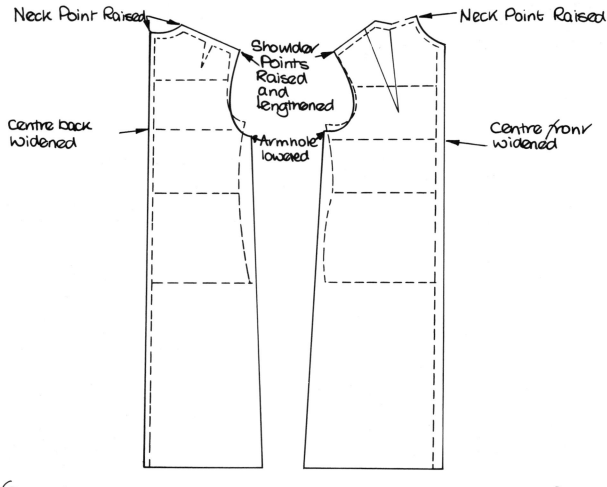

Neck Point Raised

Neck Point Raised

Shoulder Points Raised and Lengthened

Centre back Widened

Centre front widened

Armhole lowered

(Dotted line represents all-in-one bodice and skirt to hip level)

Fig. 4.96 The points and areas where ease can be obtained. The broken line represents all-in-one bodice and skirt to hip level.

BLOUSES, JACKETS, COATS

The basic cut for blouses, jackets and coats is similar to that of dresses. However, extra ease is necessary for over-garments. Allow the extra ease when pinning the fabric to the stand as the garment is modelled. If you then decide additional ease is required, this can be adjusted on the flat. When providing additional ease, the increase should be in both width and depth.

Fig. 4.96
The points and areas where ease can be obtained are illustrated in Fig. 4.96. The broken line indicates the original garment. To achieve ease, add measurement to unbroken line at neck, shoulder, centre sides and armhole.

CHAPTER 5
NECKLINES

To achieve a satisfactory neckline, experiment with the stay tape on your stand. Check that the line flows over the shoulders between the back and front to give a co-ordinated neckline. If a large neckline is desired, the neckline should be tightened to prevent the bodice falling away from the body.

Built-up necklines need more fullness around the neck and a better fit is achieved if the bodice dart is taken as a whole or part into the neckline.

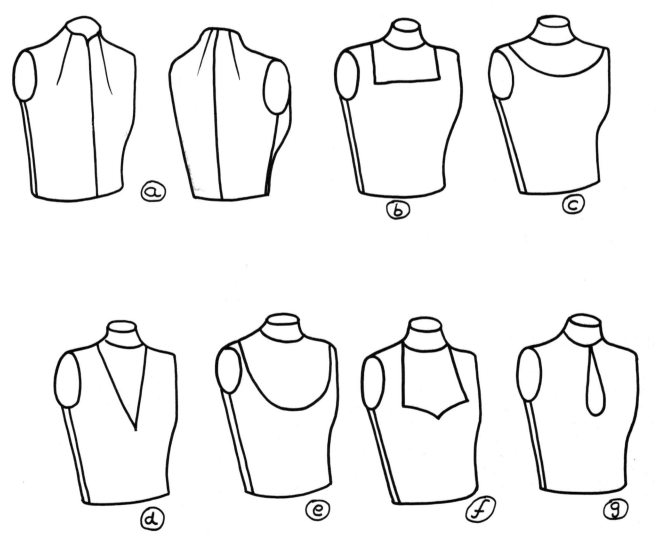

Fig. 5.1 Examples of basic necklines. (a) Built-up neckline. (b) Square. (c) Boat. (d) 'V' neckline. (e) Scoop. (f) Sweetheart. (g) Keyhole.

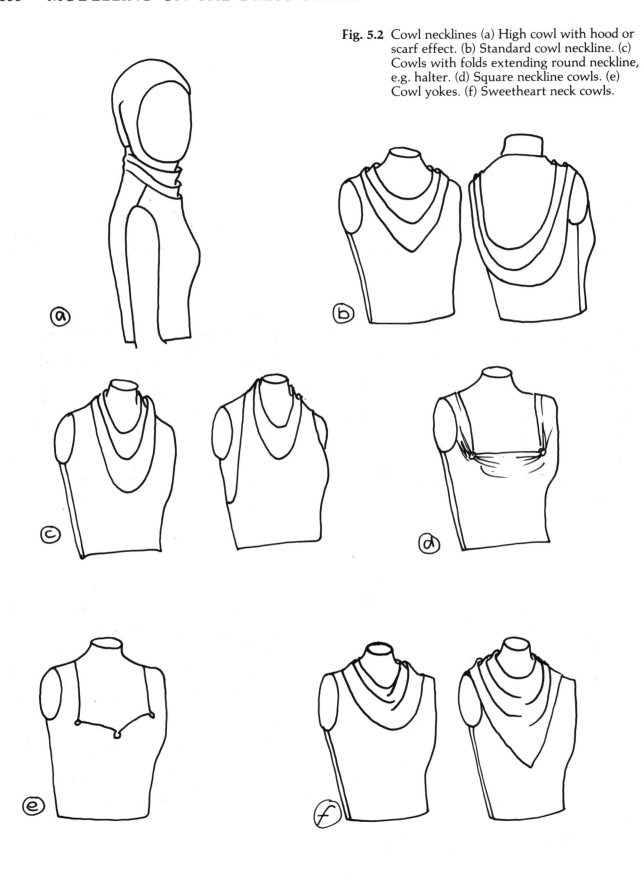

Fig. 5.2 Cowl necklines (a) High cowl with hood or scarf effect. (b) Standard cowl neckline. (c) Cowls with folds extending round neckline, e.g. halter. (d) Square neckline cowls. (e) Cowl yokes. (f) Sweetheart neck cowls.

COWL NECKLINES

Historically, a cowl was the hooded garment worn by a monk. Nowadays, it refers to any part of a garment that is draped like a hood, e.g. at armholes, hips and necklines. Cowls are best illustrated by picking up a piece of cloth by its adjacent corners; by moving these corners towards each other, a cowl drape will form. The drapes may fall casually or be precisely placed. (They are best cut on the true bias.)

Fig. 5.2
Both the depth of the neckline and each fold are determined by the amount the grain is lowered towards the centre from the outer end of the shoulder. Depending upon its depth, the cowl can take up all, part or none of the excess fabric gained from the darts. The fabric used for all drapery should have similar qualities on the warp and weft grain, in order to match the right and left side of the garment. Wide neckline cowls, or cowls at both the front and back, should be mounted on a fitted bodice in order to keep them in position.

(a) High cowl with hood or scarf effect

Fig. 5.3
The simplest form of cowl is the high cowl which gives a hood or scarf effect. This is simply made from a tube of material which fits the neckline. It can be made singly with an extension for a facing or can be cut double and folded to gain double thickness.

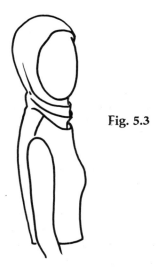

Fig. 5.3

Procedure

Follow standard preparatory stages previously described.

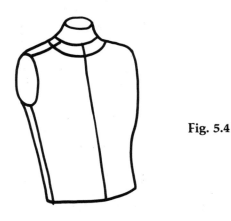

Fig. 5.4

Fig. 5.4
Tape your stand – centre front, centre back, shoulder, neckline.

A minimum circumference of 61 cms (24″) should be allowed. Do not allow tape to drop too much on back neck.

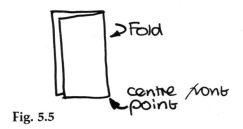

Fold

centre front point

Fig. 5.5

Fig. 5.5
Select and prepare your material as previously described

Cut fabric the size of neckline and seam allowance by the depth of collar required and seams.

Fold over fabric in half lengthwise and mark centre front point on the fold. Pin collar down centre back seam.

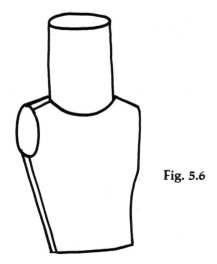

Fig. 5.6

Fig. 5.6
Place and pin material onto stand in the following way

Match centre front and centre back collar with taped centre lines on stand. Pin round on taped neckline.

Mark in balance marks on collar at shoulder seam and centre front positions.

Now follow stages 6–11 previously described in Chapter 3.

(b) Standard cowl necklines

Procedure

Follow standard preparatory stages previously described.
A whole bodice is modelled.

Fig. 5.7
Tape your stand – centre front, centre back, side seams, cowl drapes, waistline, shoulders, armhole and any dart position (if cowl is deep, darts may not be needed as the excess will be taken up by the cowl). As the centre is placed on the bias grain, a French dart is suitable as it will fall nearer the warp grain and not pull.

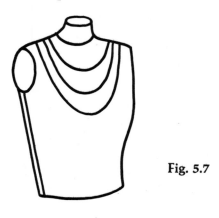

Fig. 5.7

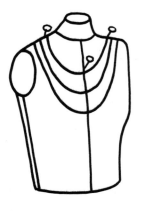

Fig. 5.8

Fig. 5.8
Select and prepare your material as previously described

Place a pin at right angles to the stand on the shoulders and centre front. Mark the centre of fabric down the lengthwise grain. (If actual fabric is used, do not mark with chalk but tack in thread.)

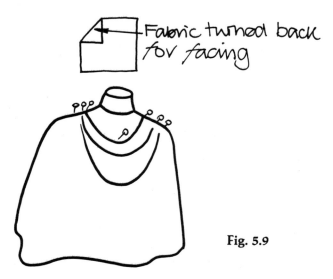

Fabric turned back for facing

Fig. 5.9

Fig. 5.9
Place and pin material onto stand in the following way

Turn back a corner of the fabric for the facing then place the centre of the fabric to the stand, matching the centre mark to the centre pin and drape neckline, pinning at both shoulders.

Allow the fabric to fall as it will. Do not stretch it. Cowls form when the fabric lies on the stand. The higher the neckline, the shallower the cowl will be. To achieve extra depth and drapes, additional fabric is raised towards the shoulders and pinned. Make sure the centre of the cowl is in line with the taped centre of stand.

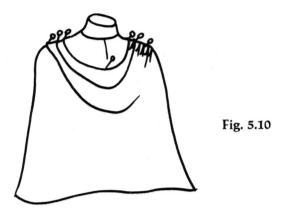

Fig. 5.10

Fig. 5.10
Additional drapes can be achieved by forming folds
or gathers at the shoulders.

Fig. 5.11

Fig. 5.11
Model the rest of the bodice as desired. Leave on
stand and model back as desired. If there is a back
cowl or wide neckline, it is best to mount the bodice
onto a plain bodice to keep the neckline in position
and prevent it slipping off the shoulders.

Mark only one side of bodice. (If garment fabric
is used, mark with pins which should lie in the
same direction as the seams, darts and folds.)

Now follow stages 6–11 as previously described
in Chapter 3.

Note: As a whole bodice has been modelled there
may be some discrepancy between the left and
right side. Choose the better one and transfer all
marking to the other side. (Leave an extended
facing of approximately 5 cms (2″) at neckline.)

Small weights may be attached to the inside of
the folds to hold them in place.

(c) Cowl with folds extending all round neckline

Procedure

Follow standard preparatory stages previously
described.

Fig. 5.12

Fig. 5.12
Tape your stand – centre front, centre back, side
seams, cowl drapes, waistline, shoulders, armhole
and any dart position.
Select and prepare your material as previously described

Fig. 5.13

Fig. 5.13
Place and pin material onto stand in the following way

Follow the stages previously described in the
former example, but wrap the neckline round to
the centre back and pin.

Note: In the previous example the neckline was
wrapped to the shoulder position only.

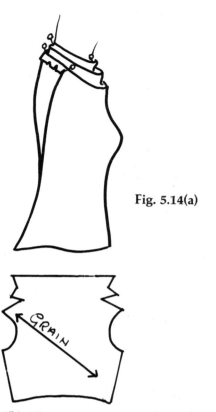

Fig. 5.14(a)

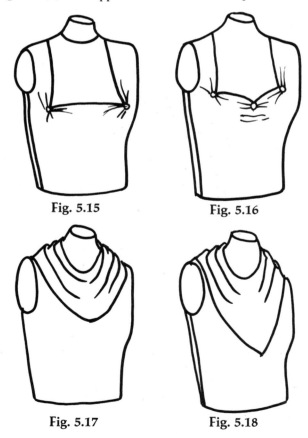

Fig. 5.14(b) The approximate resultant shape.

Fig. 5.14(a)
Nick into back neckline and at the shoulder and neck intersection. This releases excess fabric for the cowl. Additional drapes can be attained by lifting the fabric at centre front and moving the excess to the centre back. If desired, more cowls may be modelled into the shoulder seam.

Model rest of bodice as desired. Figure 5.14(b) shows the approximate resultant shape.

Now follow same procedure as described in previous example.

(d) Square neckline cowl

Fig. 5.15
A square neckline cowl is modelled as for a standard cowl, dropping the depth of neckline to the desired position and holding squareness by the use of decorative clasps, buttons, etc.

(e) Sweetheart neck cowl

Fig. 5.16
A sweetheart neck cowl is produced as a square neckline cowl, pulled down at the centre front and caught.

(f) Cowl set into a yoke

Figs. 5.17 and 5.18
A cowl may be set into any shape of yoke although a square yoke goes against the line of cowl drapes and is therefore best avoided. By setting a cowl into a yoke, a combination of deep cowls with a high neckline can be obtained, leaving the bodice to be as close fitting as desired. This avoids folds occurring at bust level.

It may not always be suitable to have the lower part of the garment on the bias, whereas the cowl should be. By setting the cowl into a yoke, it eliminates the need to put the whole garment on the bias.

Procedure

Tape your stand as for cowl and yokes, then follow stages previously described for both cowls and yokes.

Fig. 5.15   Fig. 5.16

Fig. 5.17   Fig. 5.18

CHAPTER 6
COLLARS

Modelling is by far the quickest method of producing a collar. If a collar is cut on the flat, check it on the dress stand to see it 'in the round' and view it on plan. Get the neckline and collar flowing round rather than going from point to point on the shoulder.

There are many types of collars and the way they lie depends upon collar shape and neckline.

BASIC PRINCIPLES

(1) If the same curve as the neckline is used on the inner edge of the collar, then the collar will lie flat on the garment with no stand.
(2) If the inner edge of the collar is straightened, the stand of the collar will increase and shorten the outside edge.
(3) If the outside edge of the collar is greater than the circumference round the neckline, the collar will flute.

Terms

Fig. 6.1
Neckline – line where collar is joined to neck.
Outer edge of collar – the opposite side to the neck edge.
Roll line – where the collar rolls over.

Stand – distance between neckline and height of collar.
Fall – distance between height of collar and outer edge.
Break point – change of angle from neckline to edge of button stand.
Break line – line where rever rolls back.
Button stand – distance between centre of button and edge of garment.

Collars can either be single and edged or double, being made up of under and top collar pieces. The under collar should be produced on the stand but the top collar should be built up on the flat, since it is the under collar which controls the shape. The collar should be interfaced before replacing on the stand. Once placed, decide on the size and shape of the outer edge. Any change in the width of collar will affect the stand of the collar, i.e. narrowing the collar will lower it, while widening the collar will raise the stand. Make the under collar smaller by approximately 0.5 cms (¼") – 1 cm (⅜") depending on the thickness of the fabric and type of collar. This allows the top collar to roll over without the outer seam showing. The reduction of the bottom collar is assessed when the collar is placed on the stand. A smooth roll will be achieved if the under collar is cut on the bias. The stand of the collar is reduced if the collar is cut on the bias, rather than the warp grain.

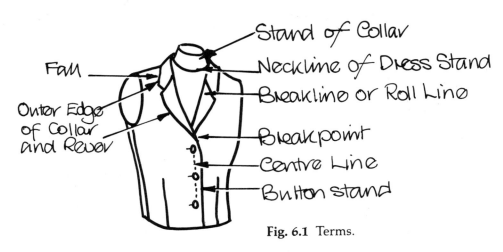

Fall

Outer Edge of Collar and Rever

Stand of Collar

Neckline of Dress Stand

Breakline or Roll Line

Breakpoint

Centre Line

Button stand

Fig. 6.1 Terms.

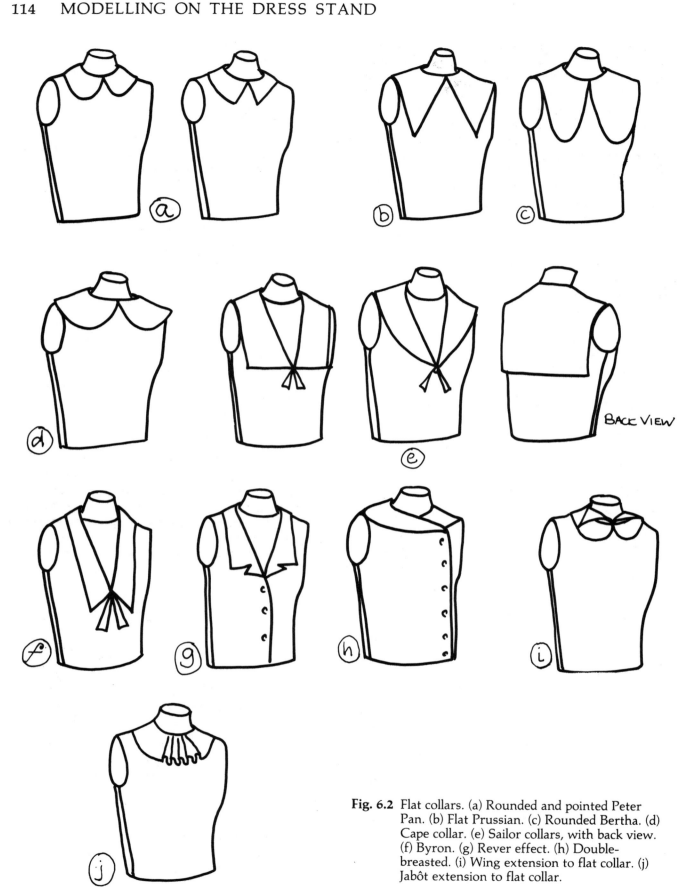

Fig. 6.2 Flat collars. (a) Rounded and pointed Peter Pan. (b) Flat Prussian. (c) Rounded Bertha. (d) Cape collar. (e) Sailor collars, with back view. (f) Byron. (g) Rever effect. (h) Double-breasted. (i) Wing extension to flat collar. (j) Jabôt extension to flat collar.

The amount the grain is lifted or dropped along the neckline of the stand from the shoulder point to the centre back affects the height of the collar roll and the distance round the outer edge of the collar. For a higher roll, the fabric must be lowered below the neck seam line of the dress stand.

When the collar is placed on the stand, any alterations required to obtain fit are achieved by darting out excess from the outer edge, or splitting and spreading, then inserting wedges of fabric to gain extra on the outer edges. A bulging collar indicates that you have over-raised the grain. A tight collar indicates that you have dropped the grain too much.

Collars fall into six categories:

(1) flat collars;
(2) fluted collars;
(3) collars with roll;
(4) stand collars;
(5) rever collars;
(6) collars all-in-one with bodice.

We shall take each of these categories in the order listed.

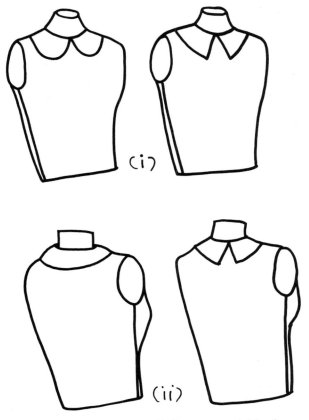

Fig. 6.3 Peter Pan collars: (i) front view, (ii) back view.

(1) FLAT COLLARS

Fig. 6.2

(a) Peter Pan collar

Fig. 6.3
A Peter Pan collar is a small flat collar with either rounded or pointed ends and can be cut in one or two pieces.

Fig. 6.4

Procedure

Fig. 6.4
Tape your stand – centre front, centre back, shoulders, neckline and outer edge of collar.
Select and prepare your material as previously described
   Note: If your fabric has a torn edge it will make your collar pucker, therefore it is necessary to proceed along the lengthwise grain by cutting a smooth edge.
Place and pin material onto stand in the following way

Centre Back Line of Collar

Fig. 6.5

Fig. 6.5
Pin fabric onto stand, matching the cut edge to centre back line on the stand with the collar depth hanging below the taped neckline.

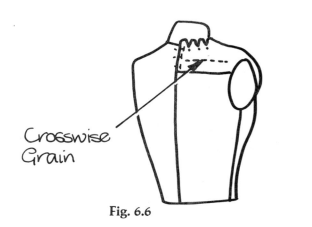

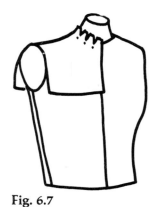

Crosswise Grain

Fig. 6.6   Fig. 6.7   Fig. 6.8

Fig. 6.6
Mark in the crosswise grain on the collar and ensure it is at right angles to the centre back line. Smooth the fabric round the neckline, pinning, nicking approximately every 2.5 cms (1″) and cutting away surplus fabric to within 1 cm (½″)

Fig. 6.7
Continue in the same manner over the shoulder to the centre front, checking that the neckline and outer edges of the fabric lie flat to the stand. The neckline should be slightly stretched.

Fig. 6.8
Mark in the desired outer edge of the collar and neckline. Place a balance mark at the shoulder seam intersection.

Collar stage A. Remove collar from stand.
Collar stage B. Press.
Collar stage C. Using modelled half collar as a pattern, cut out a full collar. Try on stand. If satisfied with result, transfer shape to a paper pattern, truing lines and checking details. Your under collar pattern will be the same as the modelled piece. Your top collar will have ¼ cm (⅛″) added above the neckline for a very slight roll to cover the neck seam.

Cutting out under and top collar

Fig. 6.9
Using paper pattern, cut out collars in fabric marking in centre back and shoulder balance marks.

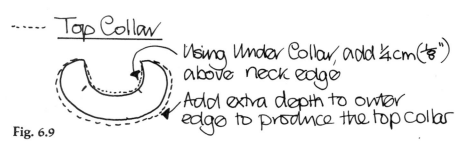

----- Top Collar

Using Under Collar, add ¼cm (⅛″) above neck edge

Add extra depth to outer edge to produce the top collar

Fig. 6.9

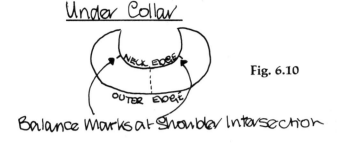

Under Collar

Fig. 6.10

Balance Marks at Shoulder Intersection

Fig. 6.10
Attach interlining to under collar with the grain in the same direction, and check on stand. If satisfied, try top collar over under collar on stand and check for amount of roll required. Now follow stages 6–11 as previously described in Chapter 3.

Other flat collars

The flat Prussian collar, rounded or square Bertha and cape collars are modelled in exactly the same way. The only difference is the shape on the outer edge. Capes themselves are modelled in the same way, but lengthened all the way round.

Flat collars with V necks, such as the sailor collar, Byron or rever effect, have the neckline taped onto the stand and then modelled in the same manner as the Peter Pan.

A flat collar may be put onto a single-buttoned bodice or double-breasted bodice. If it is single-breasted, the collar finishes at the centre front in the normal way, whereas if it is double-breasted (as in style (h)) it will be modelled round to the edge of the button stand.

Buttons and button stands

The size of button determines the width of button stand. From the centre front line, measure outwards to the extent of your button stand, the radius of the button plus at least ½ cm (¼"). Buttons push themselves to the end of the button-holes, so on a horizontal buttonhole take ¼ cm (⅛") beyond the centre front line and the remainder away from it. Starting with the button diameter as your buttonhole size for flat buttons, increase the hole size to accommodate dome-shaped buttons.

When using a panel, buttonholes should fall vertically otherwise the button would slip to the end of the button and lie beyond the edge of the panel.

Whenever possible, a button should be placed where stress occurs. On a bodice, the greatest

stress is on the bust line. A button should not be placed underneath a belt. The larger the button, the greater the distance should be allowed between buttons. Looped buttons need a button stand on the underside only.

Approximate Resultant Shape

Fig. 6.11 Style (i). Wing extension to flat collar.

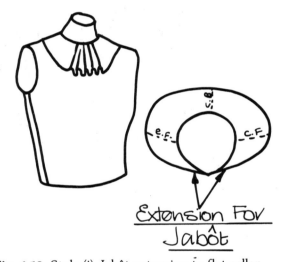

Extension For Jabôt

Fig. 6.12 Style (j). Jabôt extension to flat collar.

Variations of flat collars

By experimenting, many variations can be achieved whilst modelling. Styles (i) and (j) show two such effects.

Style (i) (Fig. 6.11) shows a wing extension to the Peter Pan. This collar is modelled as for a Peter Pan collar, but by nicking into the neckline approximately 2 cms (¾") towards the front of the shoulder seam and folding the fabric over the neck edge a winged effect is formed on top of the collar.

Style (j) (Fig. 6.12) shows a jabôt extension to the flat collar. If the fabric is allowed to continue beyond the centre front on the inner and outer edges it will give a fluted effect at the front.

(2) FLUTED COLLARS

Fig. 6.13
The fluted collar can be placed on any kind of neckline and can be extended into a wrap-over effect (see style (c)).

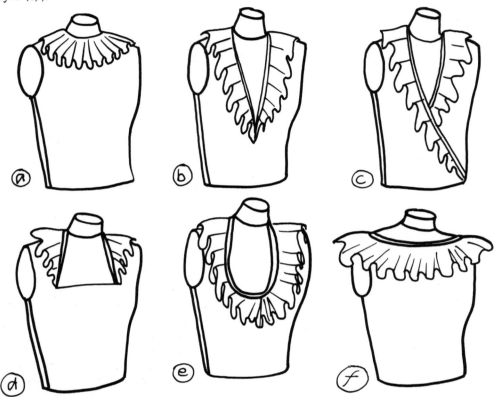

Fig. 6.13 Fluted collars, styles (a)–(f).

Style (b)

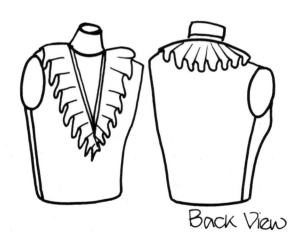

Back View

Fig. 6.14

Fig. 6.15

Procedure

Fig. 6.15
Tape your stand – centre front, centre back, shoulders, neckline and outer edge of collar.
Select and prepare your material as previously described
Allow enough material for collar width and flutings.
Place and pin material onto stand in the following way

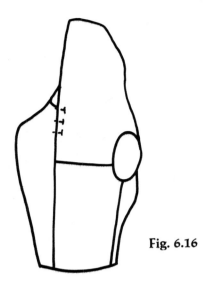

Fig. 6.16

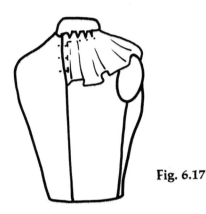

Fig. 6.17

Fig. 6.18

Fig. 6.16
Pin fabric onto stand matching the cut edge to centre back line of the stand, with the collar depth hanging below the taped neckline and the bulk of the material above the neckline.

Fig. 6.17
Mark in the crosswise grain on the collar. By lowering the grain at intervals around the neck, the outside edge of the collar will flute. (This procedure is like that done to produce flares in a circular skirt.)

Decide where you wish the flutes to fall and how much fullness is needed. Holding the bulk of the material in your right hand, lower the crosswise grain from the centre back neck point and place a flute. Pin at neck, cut away surplus to within 1 cm (½″) and nick to pin.

Continue in this way round the neck till centre front is reached. Each flute can be set and controlled separately. The more the grain is lowered, the greater the amount of fullness will fall into a flare.

Fig. 6.18
Mark in the desired outer edge of the collar and neckline. Place a balance mark at the shoulder seam intersection. Now follow collar stages A–C and general stages 6–11 previously described in Chapter 3.

The resultant shape will be circular. It may be necessary to join the collar if it is made up of more than one circle.

(3) COLLARS WITH ROLL: STYLES A – SHAPED ROLL COLLARS

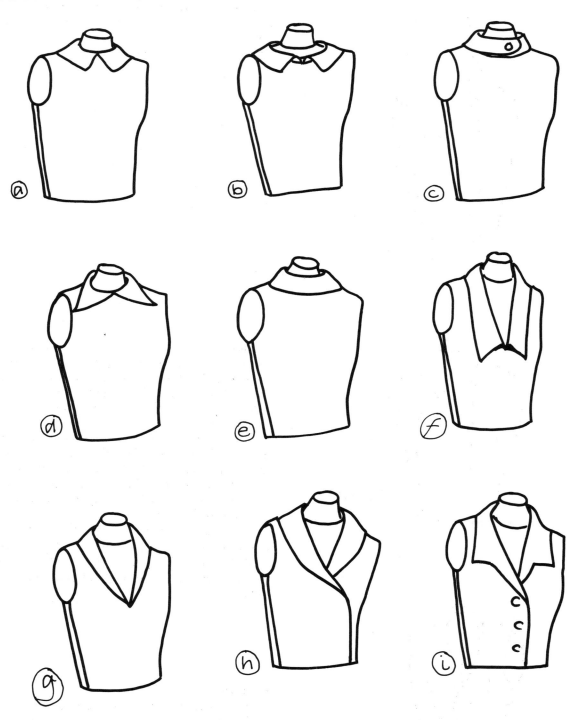

Fig. 6.19 Styles A. (a) Eton collar. (b) Roll collar with low and wide neckline. (c) Buttoned roll collar. (d) Collar with high roll at back and flat at back. (e) Roll collar. (f) High roll at back, flattening at front on a V neckline. (g) Shawl collar. (h) Double-edged shawl collar. (i) Roll collar with buttoned bodice.

Eton collar

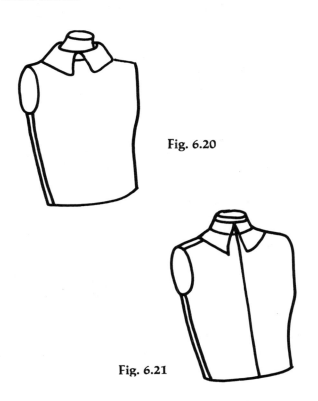

Fig. 6.20

Fig. 6.21

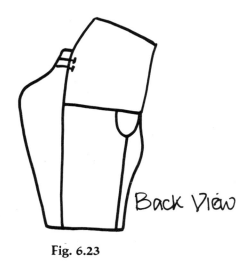

Fig. 6.23

Fig. 6.23
Pin fabric onto stand with the face of the material towards the stand as this collar will be folded over to achieve its shape, matching the cut edge to the centre back line of the stand. Pin at intersection of cut edge and neckline and on the taped line representing the height of the stand on the neck.

Procedure

Fig. 6.21
Tape your stand – centre front, centre back, shoulders, neckline, height of stand up neck, edge of collar.
Select and prepare your material as previously described

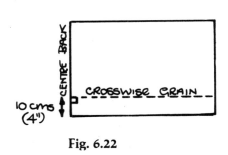

CENTRE BACK

CROSSWISE GRAIN

10 cms (4")

Fig. 6.22

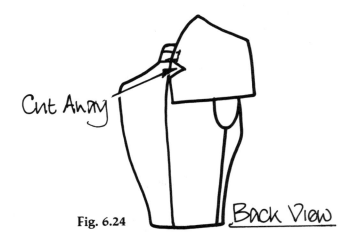

Cut Away

Fig. 6.24   Back View

Fig. 6.22
Measure up 10 cms (4") from the crosswise grain on the centre back line and draw a line at right angles.
Place and pin material onto stand in the following way

Fig. 6.24
Cut away fabric to within 1 cm (½") below the neckline at the centre back intersection, making a downward curve with the scissors and smooth fabric tightly round neck.
From top of cut, nick into neckline and pin.

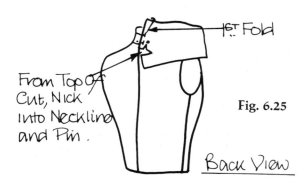

Fig. 6.25

Approximate Resultant Shape

Fig. 6.28

Fig. 6.25

Now allow the fabric to form a fold of approximately 1–2 cms (½"–1") on the top edge to nothing at the neck edge. (The higher the roll, the straighter the collar will be at the neck edge, so the crosswise grain marked on the fabric is a guide to how much roll is being added.)

Figs. 6.26, 6.27 and 6.28

Pin the fold temporarily on taped stand line. Continue round the neck to the centre front, placing three folds at centre back; near the shoulder point towards the back and halfway between the shoulder point and the centre front. Allow collar to wrap over 1 cm (½") beyond centre front line on outer edge.

Remove temporary pins holding folds and fold outer edge down over neckline. Sink pins into the stand to keep the collar on its outer edge from moving and so that the centre back remains perpendicular to the neckline.

Now follow collar stages A to C described previously in this chapter and general stages 6–11 described previously in Chapter 3.

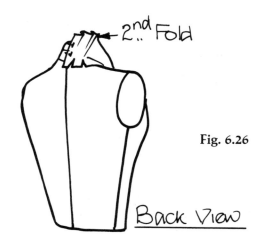

Fig. 6.26

Other shaped roll collars

The roll collar with low and wide neckline, the collar with a high roll at the back and flat at the front, and the roll collar with no neck opening are modelled following the same principles explained for the Eton collar. The varying amounts of roll can be controlled as the collar is modelled or changed as desired when seen on the stand. The collar with a high roll at the back and flat at the front will have a straight neck edge along the back of the collar and a curved one at the front (see Fig. 6.29).

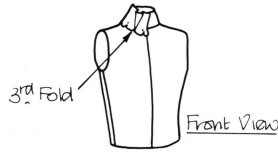

Fig. 6.27

Fig. 6.29

If the neckline has a V then that neckline is followed, but the inner edge of the collar needs to have the curve turning inwards to keep a tight outer edge.

(3) COLLARS WITH ROLL: STYLES B – BIAS FOLDED COLLARS

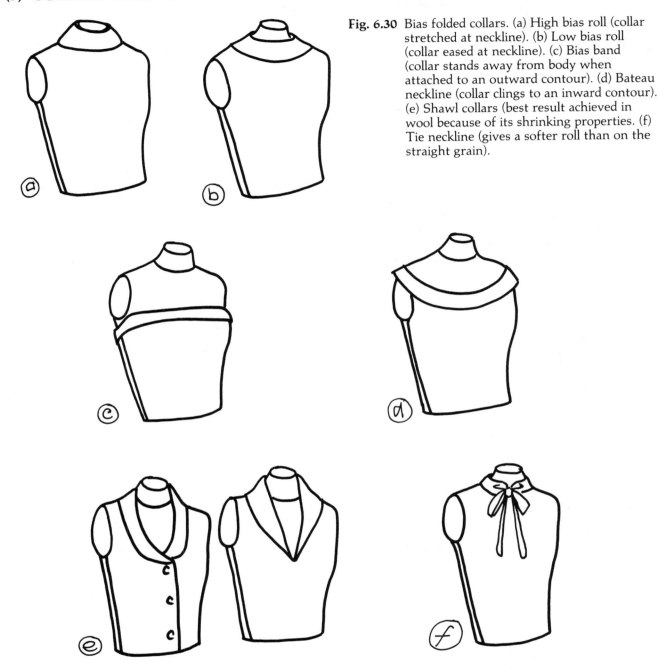

Fig. 6.30 Bias folded collars. (a) High bias roll (collar stretched at neckline). (b) Low bias roll (collar eased at neckline). (c) Bias band (collar stands away from body when attached to an outward contour). (d) Bateau neckline (collar clings to an inward contour). (e) Shawl collars (best result achieved in wool because of its shrinking properties. (f) Tie neckline (gives a softer roll than on the straight grain).

Fig. 6.30
Bias folded collars are strips of fabric cut on the true bias, folded lengthwise then stitched along the neck edge to be treated as a single thickness of collar. The success of a bias folded collar depends very much on the pliability and shrinking qualities of the fabric, and the draper's skill in manipulating and steam pressing the fabric. Cutting a collar on a bias fold makes the fabric pliable and the resultant collar lie flatter. The amount of roll varies by the amount the collar is eased or stretched onto the neckline of the bodice.

To roll close up to the neckline, the neck edge of the collar is stretched onto the neckline of the bodice. To lie flatter, the outside (i.e. the folded edge) of the collar is stretched, whilst the neck edge is eased onto the neckline of the bodice.

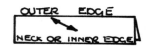

Fig. 6.31

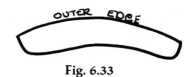

Fig. 6.33

Procedure

Fig. 6.31
Cut a rectangle of fabric on the true bias twice the width required × length of collar.

Fig. 6.32
To achieve a curved shape, a row of tacking stitches on the neck edge pulls the fabric in before shrinking by steam pressing.

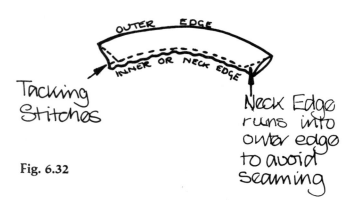

Fig. 6.32

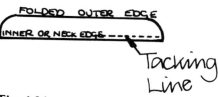

Fig. 6.34

Fig. 6.33
The seam at the end of the bias collar can be avoided by running the neck edge into the outer edge as shown.

Fig. 6.34
With neck edge shrunk and the folded edge stretched, the convex curve can be turned into a straight line.

It can be shrunk still more and form a concave curve.

(4) STAND COLLARS

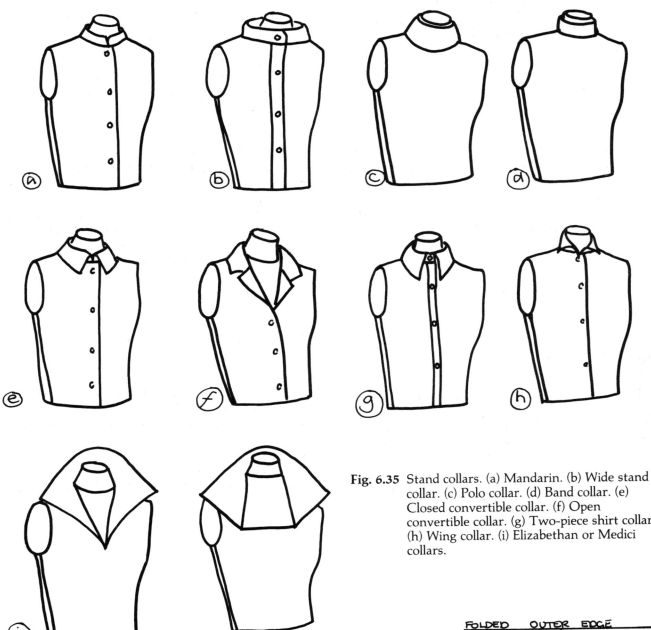

Fig. 6.35 Stand collars. (a) Mandarin. (b) Wide stand collar. (c) Polo collar. (d) Band collar. (e) Closed convertible collar. (f) Open convertible collar. (g) Two-piece shirt collar. (h) Wing collar. (i) Elizabethan or Medici collars.

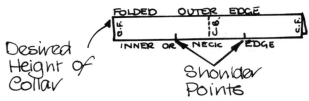

Fig. 6.36

Figs. 6.35 and 6.36
Stand collars are basically rectangles the size of the neckline by the desired height of the collar doubled over.

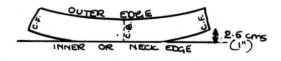

Fig. 6.37

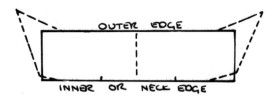

Fig. 6.38 Approximate shape of shirt or convertible collar.

Fig. 6.37
Since the circumference at the base of the neck is greater than the measurement 2.5 cm (1″) above it, if the stand collar is to cling to the neck the measurement on the outer (upper) edge of the collar has to be reduced by having a convex curve on the neck edge approximately 2.5 cms (1″) up from the base line. This is achieved by lowering the grain slightly.

Fig. 6.38
If the edge of the collar must stand away from the neck, e.g. in the Elizabethan collar, the circumference on the outer edge needs to increase. Within this group are the turn-down collars, e.g. the shirt or convertible collar which stands up the neck and then 'turns down' over a crease line (rather than a roll line) giving it a much sharper edge. The basic shape, however, is still a straight band.

Mandarin or Chinese collar

Fig. 6.39
This collar may be made to stand away from the neck at the outer edge by simply cutting it as a basic rectangle the size of the neckline plus twice the desired height of the stand. Conversely, it may be shaped to cling to the neck. Sometimes the centre front edges of a Mandarin collar meet, sometimes a gap is left. We shall model the Mandarin collar which clings to the neck and meets at the centre front edges.

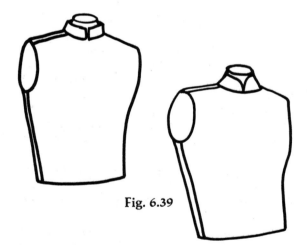

Fig. 6.39

Fig. 6.40

Procedure

Fig. 6.40
Tape your stand – centre back line of neck, centre front line of neck, shoulders, neckline, height of stand up neckline (outer edge of collar). Button stand if part of design.

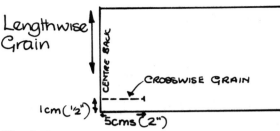

Fig. 6.41

Back View

Fig. 6.42

Back View

Fig. 6.43

Front View

Fig. 6.44

Fig. 6.41

Select and prepare your material as previously described
Before modelling onto the stand, mark in the crosswise grain from the cut edge approximately 1 cm (½") above the bottom of your piece of muslin for 5 cms (2") out.

Place and pin material onto stand in the following way

Fig. 6.42
Pin the cut edge to centre back line of neck of stand allowing 1 cm (½") of fabric below the neckline.

Fig. 6.43
Smooth out from the centre backline, keeping the marked crosswise grain on the taped neckline for 5 cms (2").

Pin and nick round neckline.

Pin and nick to within 1 cm (½") round the collar stand line for 5 cms (2").

Fig. 6.44
Now lower the crosswise grain, remembering that the more it is lowered the closer the fit at the outer edge. If the collar is to stand away from the neck, the grain should not be lowered.

If an Elizabethan collar is being modelled, the grain would be raised to make the collar fan out from the neckline. (It must also be modelled in a stiff fabric to hold its shape.) Work round to the centre front, lowering the grain, smoothing the fabric round the neck, pinning, and cutting away surplus material to within 1 cm (½") of finished shape.

By the time you reach the centre front neckline, the crosswise grain at the lower edge of the collar will be between 1 cm (½") – 4 cms (1½") above that at the centre back.

A balance mark is placed at the intersection of the neckline and shoulder line. The approximate resultant shape of the collar is shown in Fig. 6.45.

Now follow collar stages A–C and general stages 6–11 previously described in Chapter 3.

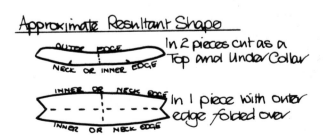

Fig. 6.45

Wing collar

Fig. 6.46

Fig. 6.48

Fig. 6.46
A wing collar fits round the neck like the Mandarin collar, but rolls over at the upper edge at the side front and turns over at the centre front.

It is modelled in exactly the same way as the Mandarin collar but the grain is lowered less from the shoulder intersection to the centre front. This avoids the upper edge becoming too tight.

Band collar

Fig. 6.47

Fig. 6.47
The band collar resembles the Mandarin collar but the opening is at the back. It is modelled from the front to the back.

Convertible collar

A convertible collar is one that can be worn open or closed (e.g a shirt collar). In order that the collar may cling to the neck when open or closed, the neckline of the collar needs to have a convex curve. It can be cut as a basic rectangle but it is better if it has an inward curve from the centre back to

approximately 2.5cms (1") in front of the shoulder seam intersection then straightened off to the breakline of the rever.

This collar is set on to a standard neckline with a button stand.

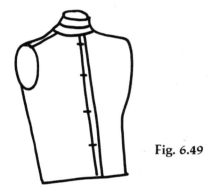

Fig. 6.49

Procedure

Fig. 6.49
Tape your stand – centre front, button stand, position of buttons, centre back, shoulders, neckline, collar stand.

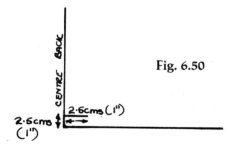

Fig. 6.50

Fig. 6.50
Select and prepare your material as previously described
Measure up 2.5 cms (1") from the crosswise grain on the cut edge and draw a line at right angles for 2.5 cms (1"). This is where the neck starts to curve.
Place and pin material onto stand in the following way

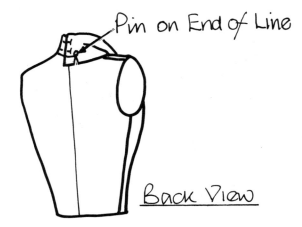

Fig. 6.51

Fig. 6.51
Pin fabric onto stand, matching the cut edge to the centre back line on the stand, with the crosswise marked line on the fabric on the taped neckline. Place pin on end of line and nick up to pin. On centre back line, pin fabric 2 cms (¾") – 2.5 cms (1") above neckline for the height of the stand and to hold the fabric in position.

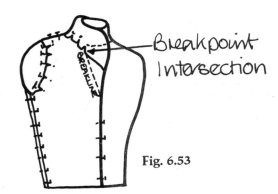

Fig. 6.53

Fig. 6.53
Turn the rever of the bodice upwards before continuing to pin the collar round the front part of the neck. Pin the collar to the neckline of the bodice, lifting the grain of the fabric approximately 2.5 cms (1") in front of the shoulder seam intersection. (A minimum of ½ cm (¼") should be allowed below the neckline for seam allowance.) Without moving the grain, continue to break line of rever. Pin and nick as you go.

Start from centre back and reverse procedure, lowering the grain in order to produce an outward curve and to tighten the outer edge of the collar. At the centre front the raw edge of the collar is approximately 2 cms (¾") below the neckline, so the grain will have dropped that amount.

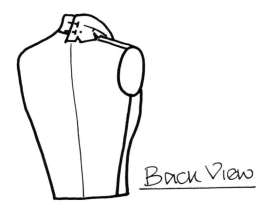

Fig. 6.52

Fig. 6.52
Lift the crosswise grain 2 cms (¾") above the taped neckline at the shoulder intersection, pin and nick. (This will produce an inward curve and will increase the ease on the outer edge of the collar.)

Fig. 6.54

Fig. 6.55

Figs. 6.54 and 6.55
Turn back the rever.

Fold the collar over and cut away surplus to desired shape on outer edge. There should be no pull on the outer edge but if it does pull, nick into the collar from the outer edge to the neck edge at the back and shoulder till the collar falls to the desired width and collar stand.

Make a note of the alterations to be corrected on the flat.

Now follow collar stages A–C and general stages 6–11 previously described in Chapter 3.

(5) REVER COLLARS

Fig. 6.56 Examples of rever collars.

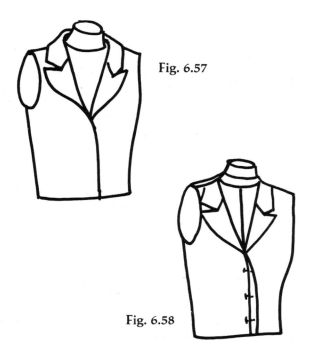

Fig. 6.57

Fig. 6.58

Modelling a rever collar

Fig. 6.57
The rever collar in its construction involves the collar and the rever which is cut all in one with the bodice. There are many variations, as illustrated, but the underlying principles in each case are the same.

Procedure
Fig. 6.58
Tape your stand – centre back line of neck, shoulders, outer edge of collar, button stand and rever, centre front line, position of buttons stand and roll line of collar.
Select and prepare your material as previously described

Bodice and Rever

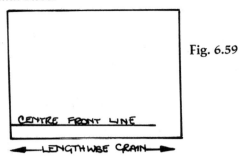

Fig. 6.59

Fig. 6.59
Estimate amount allowing for approximate extension to the width of the bodice to accommodate the rever then draw a line down the lengthwise grain in from right edge for the centre front line.
Place and pin material onto stand in the following way

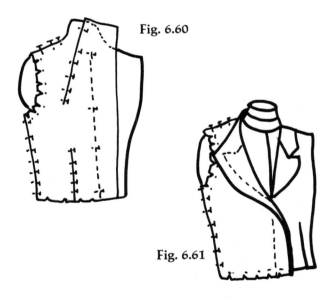

Fig. 6.60

Fig. 6.61

Fig. 6.60
Model the front bodice as desired. A neckline dart is often used in tailored jackets since most of the darts can be hidden by the rever. For this exercise, model the bodice with a neckline dart but do not cut away excess above the neckline.

Fig. 6.61
Mark the taped edge of the rever to breakpoint and down to the end of the bodice. Fold the fabric over on the roll line (breakline) for the rever, pinning it onto the stand at the shoulder position to hold it securely. Check carefully details of breakline, length and slant of seam joining rever to collar, shape and roll of rever etc.

Cut on marked outer edge from base of bodice upwards, to where collar and rever join. Mark the position of the exposed seam which joins the collar to the rever on both sides of the fabric.
Remove pin at shoulder.

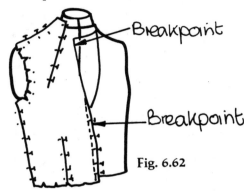

Fig. 6.62

Fig. 6.62
The remainder of the neck is best dealt with if the rever is pushed up against the neck. From the neck and shoulder intersection, blend a line into the seam which joins the collar to the rever.
Cut away surplus to within 1 cm (½″).
Mark in neckline, balance mark at shoulder seam intersection, where breaklines of collar and rever meet and the roll line of collar from centre back to the front.

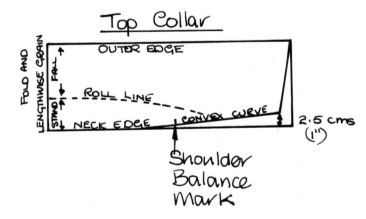

Fig. 6.63 The under collar can be cut as a pair on the bias grain with an under centre back line to help the fit.

Fig. 6.63
Now follow collar stages A–C and general stages 6–11 previously described in Chapter 3.
Note: The facing for the rever collar is cut large on the outer edge as far as the breakpoint to allow for the rever to roll over.

Fig. 6.64

Wide rever collar

Fig. 6.64
As can be seen from the flat pattern shape, the rever collar modelled results in a convex curved neckline. The stand rises as the width increases so if a wider collar is required without having the increase in stand, it can either be adjusted after it has been modelled (in the same way as in the convertible collar) or a slightly concave curve can be introduced across the back of the neckline and then into a convex curve in the modelling procedure.

(6) COLLARS ALL-IN-ONE WITH BODICE

Fig. 6.65 (*opposite*)

Modelling collars cut all-in-one with bodice

Fig. 6.66
This collar uses the excess fabric above shoulder level and within the neck area to achieve a great variety of styles. It is cut all in one piece with the front bodice extending into the back neckline. This forms the undercollar. The top collar is cut in one piece with the front facing and may have the centre back without a seam. The outer edge can be cut to any shape as shown in Fig. 6.66.

Procedure

Fig. 6.67
Tape your stand – centre front, button stand and position of buttons (if required), shoulders, neckline, centre back neck, outer edge of collar, height of stand along back neckline.
Select and prepare your material as previously described

Fig. 6.68
Decide on extension beyond the centre front to accommodate the button stand and collar. (This can be considerable if it is to be double-breasted.)
    Allow fabric above shoulder line for collar depth.
    Draw a line lengthwise along grain for the centre front.
Place and pin material onto stand in the following way
Model back bodice as desired and leave pinned to stand.

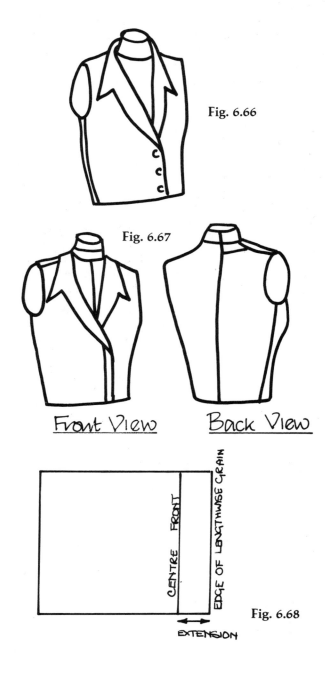

Fig. 6.66

Fig. 6.67

Front View   Back View

Fig. 6.68

EXTENSION

Fig. 6.65 Collars all-in-one with bodice. (a) Rever front. (b) Roll at back, flat in front. (c) Curls in front. (d) Rolls high back and front. (e) Combined stand and rever. (f) Roll. (g) Shawl. (h) High shaped. (i) Rever collar effect. (j) Fly-away.

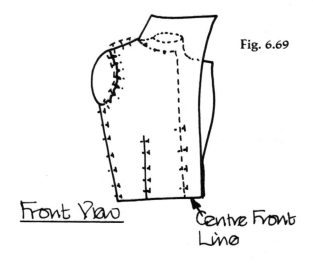

Fig. 6.69

Front View

Centre Front Line

Fig. 6.69
Model front bodice as desired leaving excess fabric beyond the shoulder, within the neck area and over the centre front line, placing the marked centre front line and button stand line on the fabric to those on the stand.

Pin at approximate bust level, waist and between these points.

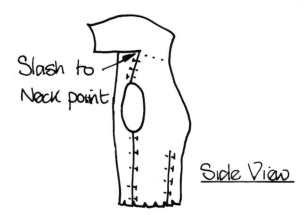

Slash to Neck point

Side View

Fig. 6.70

Fig. 6.70
Nick into desired neckpoint on the shoulder line and pin.

Turn the shoulder seam allowance in on itself.

Remove temporary pins from round neckline.

Fig. 6.71
Smooth beyond the nick to the back of the neck, allowing fabric to drop 1 cm (½″) below taped neck (for seam allowance).

Pin along back neckline and up centre back neckline to stand height, smoothing and slightly stretching it as you pin.

Fig. 6.72
Roll the fabric over on the desired breakline to the breakpoint of the button stand at the front bodice.

Pin the breakline to the side of the neck at the shoulder seam, keeping it the same height as the collar stand at the back neck. It will be seen that the height of the roll increases from the breakpoint to the shoulder.

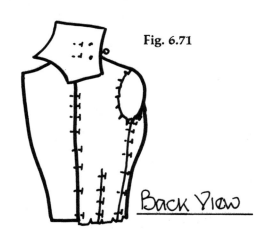

Fig. 6.71

Back View

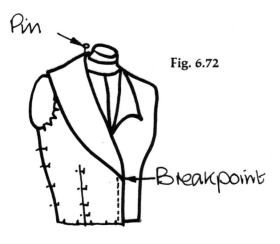

Pin

Fig. 6.72

Breakpoint

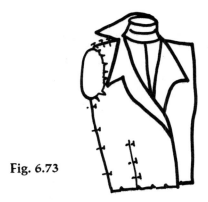

Fig. 6.73

Fig. 6.73
Mark in the desired outer edge of the front collar on the folded back fabric. Cut away surplus to this line.

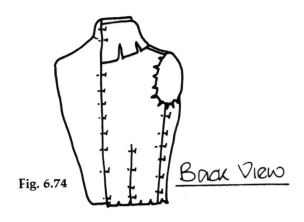

Fig. 6.74

Back View

Fig. 6.74
Continue round to back with the collar rolled over and pin to centre back neck. Keep the stand the same height as that at the neckpoint on the shoulder.

Nick into the desired width from the outer edge to allow the collar to lie smoothly.

Mark in outer edge and cut away surplus.

Mark in centre back line and cut away surplus to within 1 cm (½").

Fig. 6.75

Dart out Excess

Fig. 6.75
Remove centre back pins on folded over collar. Turn the collar upwards to see if there is excess fold along the front neckline. If there is, place a shallow dart from neck and shoulder intersection towards breakpoint.

Note: The pattern to be produced for the facing and top collar requires description as difficulty arises in keeping the grain straight in the desired positions.

Procedure

Fig. 6.76
Trace the outer edge of the toile as shown.

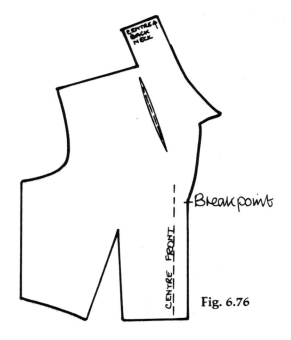

Breakpoint

Fig. 6.76

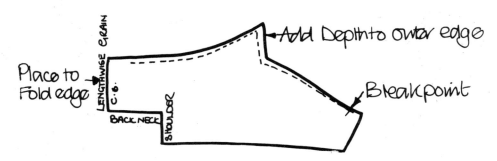

Fig. 6.77 This forms the top collar and facing combined.

Fig. 6.77
The top collar on the centre back line requires a vertical grain, which has the effect of throwing the lower part of the pattern onto the bias, introducing a join where two differing grains would meet. For this reason, we need to cut the pattern at a point just below the breakpoint, ensuring that the division does not correspond to a buttonhole position.

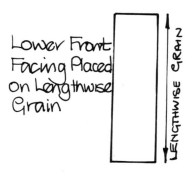

Fig. 6.78 Lower front facing placed on lengthwise grain.

Fig. 6.78
The lower part of the divided pattern is used to produce the lower facing.

The upper part of the divided pattern is used to produce the top collar and facing.

As the top collar needs to be larger than the under collar, we need to increase the pattern depth, as illustrated in Fig. 6.77.

Now follow collar stages A–C and general stages 6–11 previously described in Chapter 3.

CHAPTER 7
SLEEVES

A sleeve is probably that part of a garment which is most likely to be constructed 'on the flat' and not modelled because stands do not have arms which accurately represent reality. This situation is regretted, as modelling provides that freedom of expression in design, which is not available in constructing on the flat.

We shall show how to overcome the difficulties in modelling sleeves and, it is hoped, prove that you can model a sleeve as successfully as any other part of a garment.

There are many types of sleeve and, in very loose terms, we can classify them into those which are separate from the bodice and those which are all-in-one with the bodice. A selection of sleeve shapes in both classifications is illustrated below in Figs. 7.1 and 7.2.

SLEEVES SEPARATE FROM THE BODICE

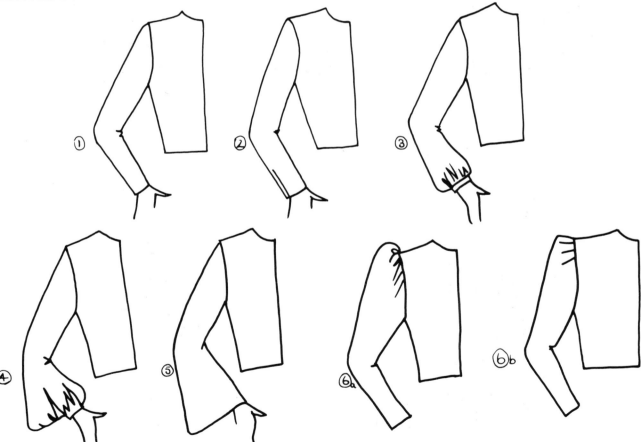

Fig. 7.1 Sleeves separate from the bodice. (1) Fitted sleeve with elbow dart. (2) Fitted sleeve with wrist dart. (3) Fitted sleeve with gathers at wrist. (4) Bishop sleeve. (5) Flared sleeve. (6) Sleeves with tucks or darts at sleeve head: (a) leg of mutton with gathers, (b) leg of mutton with tucks or darts.

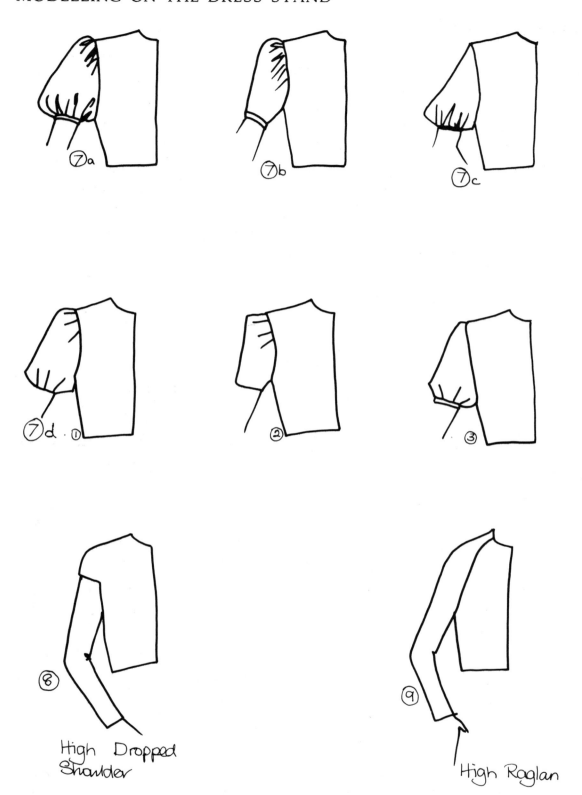

Fig. 7.1 (*cont.*) Sleeves separate from the bodice. (7) Puff sleeve: (a) with gathers at top and bottom; (b) with gathers at top only; (c) with gathers at bottom only; (d) (1) with tucks or darts top and bottom; (2) with tucks or darts at top; (3) with tucks or darts at bottom. (8) High dropped shoulder. (9) High raglan.

SLEEVES ALL-IN-ONE WITH THE BODICE

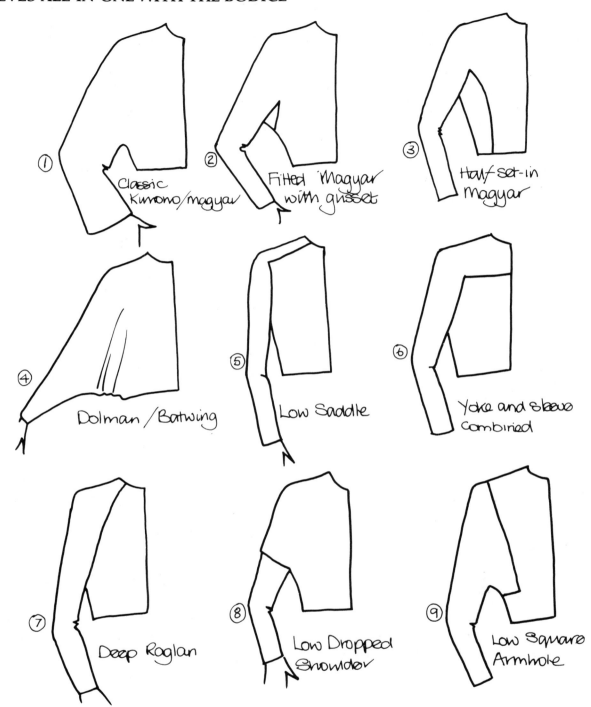

Fig. 7.2 Sleeves all in one with the bodice. (1) Classic kimono/magyar. (2) Fitted kimono/magyar with gusset. (3) Half set in kimono/magyar. (4) Dolman/batwing. (5) Low saddle. (6) Yoke and sleeve combined. (7) Deep raglan. (8) Low dropped shoulder. (9) Low square armhole.

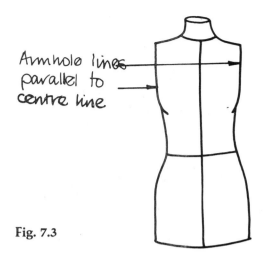

Armhole lines parallel to centre line

Fig. 7.3

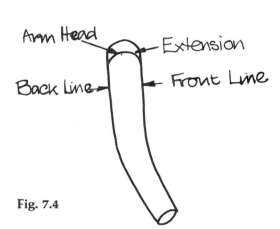

Arm Head — Extension

Back Line — Front Line

Fig. 7.4

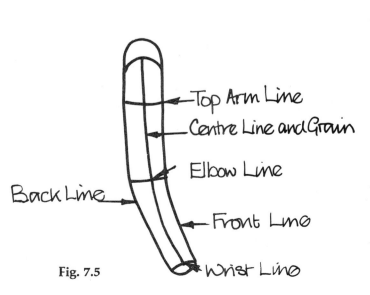

Top Arm Line

Centre Line and Grain

Elbow Line

Back Line

Front Line

Wrist Line

Fig. 7.5

PREPARATION OF ARMHOLE TO RECEIVE SLEEVE

Procedure

(1) Check the bodice armhole

Before modelling the sleeve, the rest of the garment should be placed on the stand and the armhole observed. The sleeve cannot hang properly if the armhole fits incorrectly. An incorrect fit may be caused by inadequate darting for the bust or shoulder blades, or an ill-fitting shoulder line.

Fig. 7.3
First adjust the stand so that the armhole is at eye level. Looking at the stand face on at armhole level, the armhole line should appear parallel to the centre lines of the stand.

Lower the stand in order to look at the armhole on plan, the line of which should flow continuously over the shoulder.

(2) Prepare the arm

Fig. 7.4
An attachable padded arm on which to model a sleeve can be purchased. It is covered with canvas and joined with two vertical seams positioned to correspond with the front and back line of the sleeve block. A canvas extension over the sleeve head facilitates the pinning of the arm onto the stand.

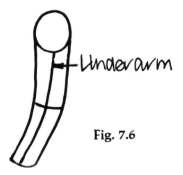

Underarm

Fig. 7.6

Taping the arm

Figs. 7.5 and 7.6
Tape over the seam lines on the arm which form the front and back lines.

Tape down the centre of the two panels. These form the centre line and underarm line.

Tape the wrist.

Tape the elbow line where the arm bends.

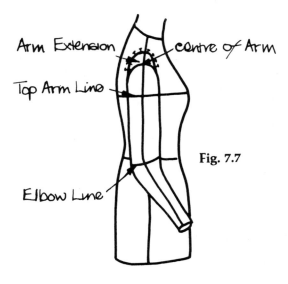

Arm Extension
Centre of Arm
Top Arm Line
Elbow Line

Fig. 7.7

Fig. 7.7
Now pin the arm onto the stand with the extension piece pinned firmly onto the shoulder, pulling it well over. The arm should swing forward. The centre line tape should fall perpendicular to the ground on the upper arm and is the grain position.

The top arm line (or crown depth, or biceps line) may now be taped. This should be in line with the underarm point of the bodice and at right angles to the centre line.

Tape the armhole line over the attached arm extension to the shoulder along the same tape as the bodice armhole.

Place the tape along the shoulder line of the stand and bring it in line with the centre of the arm in order to identify the top notch of the sleeve head.

(3) Draft the basic sleeve from the padded arm

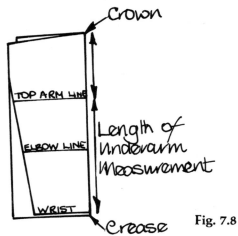

Crown
TOP ARM LINE
ELBOW LINE
WRIST
Length of underarm measurement
Crease

Fig. 7.8

Fig. 7.8
Cut a rectangle of paper approximately 69 cms × 38 cms (27″ × 15″).

Crease the paper down its centre lengthwise.

Measure down the crease the distance from the crown to the top arm line and square out from the folded edge for the top arm line to half width of top arm line.

Measure, down the crease, the underarm measurement from top arm line to wrist and square out half the width of wrist.

Now join end of squared out lines.

Establish and mark position of elbow line (this is where the arm bends forward).

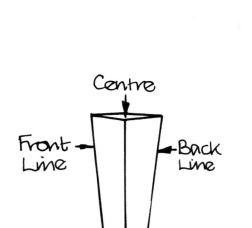

Centre
Front Line
Back Line

Fig. 7.9

Fig. 7.9
Crease the paper from the underarm seam to centre line on both sides of centre line. This indicates the position of the back and front lines.

Draw in these lines.

Now cut along outlines.

Select and prepare your material in the following way

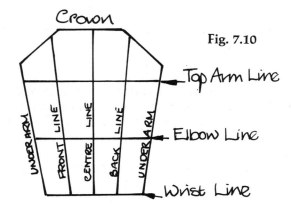

Fig. 7.10

Fig. 7.10
Using this pattern and marking in all lines, cut out in muslin, leaving approximately 2 cms (¾″) seam allowance. Cut away upper corners.
Place and pin material onto arm in the following way

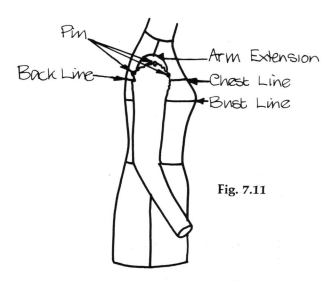

Fig. 7.11

Fig. 7.11
Pin underarm seams together and place onto arm, matching lines of toile with the tape on arm. Pin at junction of centre sleeve and shoulder seam of bodice. Pin where chest and back line meet the sleeve and mark. Keep most of the ease above these points. Compare the back armhole with the front. Note that the back is almost on the straight grain, whilst the front is on the bias.

The greater amount of ease is done in the front armhole to allow for the shoulder. This ease can be steamed away and will not be noticeable because of the bias grain of both the armhole and the sleeve head.

Unpin the underarm seam.
Press and lay toile on the flat.

Transfer the chest and back balance marks and the under-armhole curve from the bodice to the pattern draft. Now cut toile to underarm curve on pattern draft, leaving seam allowance. In order to obtain a good fit of curve, place the sleeve on a human arm with the model wearing the bodice. Now mark in the upper armhole line.

Remove from live model, press and lay on the flat.

Cut away to line, allowing 1 cm (½″) seam allowance. Make up sleeve and insert to armhole of garment toile.

(4) *Check the sleeve*

Place back on stand to check for appearance, then double check on a human figure for comfort and ease of movement. The sleeve should not be too tight in the width and should swing slightly towards the front of the body, as that is how the arm naturally falls.

Since it is the crosswise grain which controls the hang of the sleeve, check that it is neither pulling upwards nor downwards. No wrinkles should be visible.

The model should move *her* arms all around to check if *she* can do this easily.

SLEEVES CUT SEPARATE FROM THE BODICE

(1) Fitted sleeve with elbow dart

Unless the garment is to be made in a knitted fabric or is cut on the bias, consideration has to be given for the bending of the arm. Therefore, it is necessary to introduce some form of ease over the elbow – in this case an elbow dart.

Procedure

Stage 1.
Tape the arm – as for basic sleeve
Stage 2.
Select and prepare your material as previously described
The same procedure is followed as for a basic sleeve, but allow an extra 2.5 cms (1″) length to accommodate the dart.
Stage 3.
Place and pin material onto arm in the following way

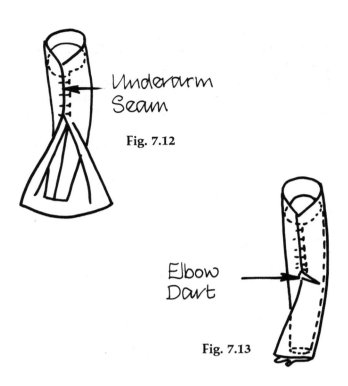

Fig. 7.12

Underarm Seam

Elbow Dart

Fig. 7.13

Fig. 7.12
Pin the underarm seam from the underarm point to the elbow line.

Fig. 7.13
Now smooth the fabric round the lower part of the arm, fitting the front of the sleeve and pinning to the taped underarm seam. Repeat fitting the back and push the excess fabric towards the elbow line in order to form a dart.

Pin out the dart then complete lower section by smoothing fabric towards underarm seam.
Stage 4. Mark in all details and remove from stand.
Stage 5. Press.
Stage 6. True all lines and check details.
Stage 7. Check seam allowances.
Stage 8. Make up and press.
Stage 9. Sew sleeve into armhole, place on stand and check for any discrepancies.

(2) Fitted sleeve with wrist dart

Underarm Seam

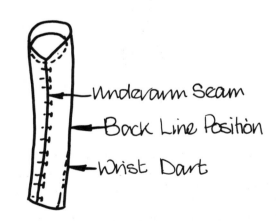

Underarm Seam
Back Line Position
Wrist Dart

Fig. 7.14

Fig. 7.14
Follow the same procedure as for sleeve with elbow dart, but allow 5 cms (2″) extra length for dart: Take the excess below the elbow level on the back line and form a dart.

(3) Fitted sleeve with gathers at wrist

Follow the same procedure described for sleeve with wrist dart, allowing extra length for blousing at wrist. More fullness is required at the back of

the sleeve for ease over the elbow. More length may be added at this point for extra ease if the sleeve is to be attached to a fitted cuff.

Procedure

Tape the arm – as for basic sleeve.
Select and prepare your material as previously described
Allow extra length for blousing of gathers.
Place and pin material onto arm in the following way

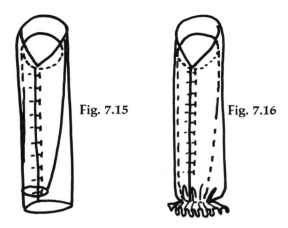

Fig. 7.15   Fig. 7.16

Fig. 7.15
Proceed as for sleeve with wrist dart missing the
dart and pin the sleeve all the way along the
underarm seam.

Fig. 7.16
After sleeve has been removed from stand, match
underarm seam and gather base of sleeve. Fit
onto a human model's arm. If more gathering is
required, the underarm seam can be unpicked and
a wedge of fabric inserted from bottom to top of
sleeve to the amount required.

Now follow stages 4–9 previously described in
fitted sleeve with elbow dart.

(4) Bishop sleeve and (5) flared sleeve

Bishop and flared sleeves are produced following
the same method, but adding extra fullness at the
sides. If enough fullness cannot be obtained by
adding at the sides, then a wedge of material can be
inserted by slitting along the centre line.

(6) Leg of mutton sleeves

(a) *with gathers*

A leg of mutton sleeve is basically a fitted sleeve
with a gathered head. The fullness may start at any
level above the elbow. The lower part of the sleeve
is modelled in the same way as the fitted sleeve
with elbow dart, but the fabric needs to be cut
wider and longer to allow for the gathered upper
section.

Procedure

Tape your stand – as for basic sleeve plus level above
elbow where you wish fullness to start.
Select and prepare your material in the following way

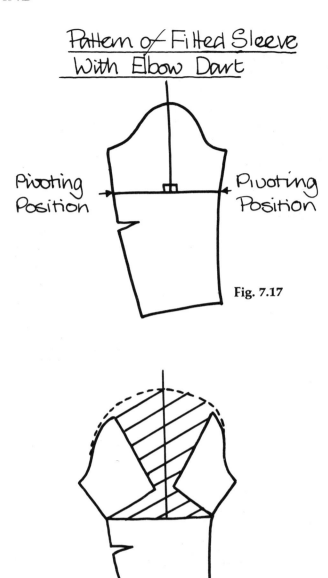

Pattern of Fitted Sleeve
With Elbow Dart

Pivoting
Position   Pivoting
                        Position

Fig. 7.17

Fig. 7.18

Figs. 7.17 and 7.18
The pattern of the fitted sleeve with elbow dart
may be traced off and an inverted 'T' shape cut into
the pattern from the centre sleeve head to the
depth required for the gathered top section, then
squared out to underarm seam. This is then spread
out using the underarm seam points as pivoting
points.

Estimate the amount of fullness required, trace
off and cut out. The resultant shape will look
similar to that shown in the illustration.
Place and pin material onto arm in the following way:

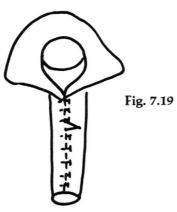

Fig. 7.19

Fig. 7.19
Model lower section of sleeve.

Fig. 7.20
Gather top of sleeve head, keeping gathering away from lower section.

Place on arm and attach arm to stand.

Arrange gathers, checking that the sleeve head is the same measurement as the armhole.

If any alteration to the amount of gathering is needed, then follow the procedure for drafting the original shape.

Fig. 7.20

Now follow stages 4–9 previously described in fitted sleeve with elbow dart.

(b) Fitted sleeve with darts or tucks in sleeve head

The only difference in procedure with this sleeve and the former one is that it is imperative that the position and direction of the darts or tucks are clearly indicated and the amount of fullness in each dart or tuck is established.

(7) Puff sleeves

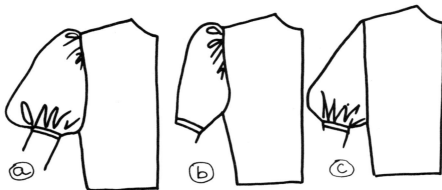

Fig. 7.21 Puff sleeve gathered (a) at the head and bottom, (b) at the head, or (c) at the bottom only.

Fig. 7.21
A puff sleeve is a short sleeve which may be (a) gathered at the head and the bottom, (b) gathered at the head only, or (c) gathered at the bottom only.

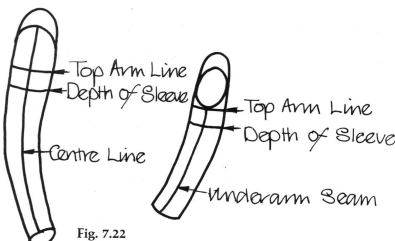

Fig. 7.22

Procedure

Fig. 7.22

Tape your stand – centre line, underarm seam, top arm line, depth of sleeve.

Select and prepare your material

Cut fabric to full width and depth required allowing extra for take up of gathers (see Fig. 7.23).

Mark in vertical centre line.

Fold fabric over on this line and cut out roughly the shape.

Machine gather sleeve head, if required, from approximately 10 cms (4″) from the underarm seam.

Sew underarm seams together.

Press open.

Place and pin fabric onto stand in the following way

Fig. 7.24

Pin head of centre vertical line to shoulder of bodice and underarm point of sleeve to that of bodice side seam.

Adjust the gathering around the sleeve head so that the sleeve head measurement equals that of

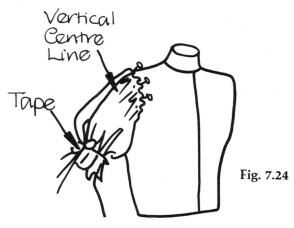

Fig. 7.24

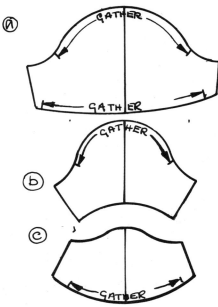

Fig. 7.23 (a) Gathers top and bottom. (b) Gathers at top only. (c) Gathers at bottom only.

the armhole.

For the gathering around the bottom, tie a tape over the sleeve at the level taped on the arm. Ease fabric up over the tape to allow for blousing and arrange gathers. Make a note of the size of tape for either cuff measurement or binding.

If style (b) or (c) is required, eliminate the gathering where the sleeve is fitted.

Mark in all details including balance marks.

Remove sleeve from arm. Unpick underarm seam.

On the flat, the sleeve shape from the underarm seam to approximately 7.5 cms (3″) up the sleeve head should be cut the same shape as the armhole curves on the front and back bodice.

Now follow stages 4–9 previously described in fitted sleeve with elbow dart.

(8) High drop shoulder

A high drop shoulder has the bodice section extending into the sleeve on or above the back and chest levels. The sleeve head is on the bodice.

Any design may be used for the lower section of the sleeve.

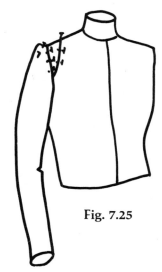

Fig. 7.25

Procedure

Fig. 7.25

Place a made-up plain sleeve over the arm.

Attach the arm to the stand as previously described, allowing the arm to fall naturally by the side of the stand.

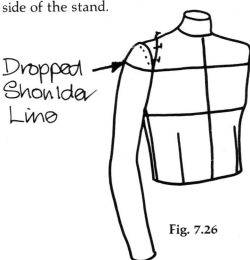

Fig. 7.26

Fig. 7.26

Tape the stand – centre front, centre back, side seam, chest, backline, neckline, waistline, armhole, darts or style lines of bodice, the dropped shoulder line (which should be on or above the chest level), the length of sleeve.

Select and prepare your material as previously described

Allow enough width of material for the extension over the shoulder point for the dropped shoulder line.

Place and pin material onto stand in the following way

Fig. 7.27

Fig. 7.27

Follow the procedure previously described for a bodice extending over the arm to the taped line. (The amount of sleeve head put onto the bodice is removed from the sleeve.)

Back bodice

Follow the same procedure as for front, matching the shoulder line.

Now follow stages 4–9 previously described in fitted sleeve with elbow dart.

Approximate resultant shape

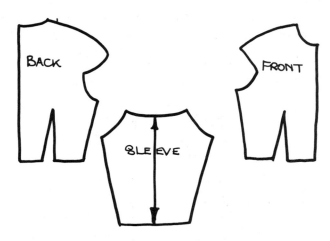

Fig. 7.28 Approximate resultant shape.

Variations of high dropped shoulder

Fig. 7.29 Variations of high dropped armhole.

(9) High raglan sleeve

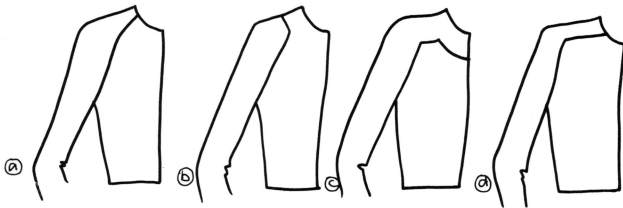

Fig. 7.30 High raglan sleeve: (a) extending into neck; (b) extending into shoulder; (c) extending into a yoke; (d) saddle shoulder.

A raglan sleeve is attached to the bodice by a diagonal seam which runs from the underarm towards the neck. The sleeve can be cut in either one piece or two pieces – a front and back sleeve. Various styles can be achieved as illustrated in Fig. 7.30.

The high raglan sleeve is high at the armhole whilst falling smoothly along the shoulder.

Procedure

Just as the high drop shoulder is based on the principle of removing one part of the garment and adding it on to the adjoining part, so it is with the high raglan. This time it is part of the bodice which is added to the sleeve.

Attach arm to stand.
Tape your stand – shoulder line, underarm seam, centre lines, waistline, raglan line and length of sleeve required on arm.
Select and prepare your material as previously described
Allow enough width for the extension of the sleeve into the bodice.
Place and pin material onto stand in the following way

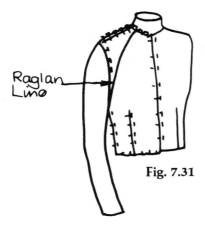

Fig. 7.31

Fig. 7.31
Make up and place on the stand the basic bodice block and the fitted sleeve block. Join together and place on the stand.

Mark in taped lines and all details onto muslin. Remove from stand.

Cut along shoulder line and unpick underarm seam in order for the muslin to lie flat.

Note: In style (b) – extending into shoulder – when the sleeve is removed from the bodice it will be necessary to nick several times into the sleeve head from the style line for it to lie flat. This will make the distance across the seam greater on the sleeve than on the bodice. The excess will have to be eased and steamed into the bodice seam to which it is attached.

Approximate resultant shapes for raglan extending into neck

Fig. 7.32 Approximate resultant shapes for raglan extending into neck.

Approximate resultant shapes for raglan extending into shoulder

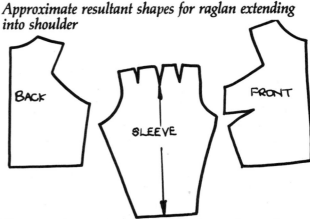

Fig. 7.33 Approximate resultant shapes for raglan extending into shoulder.

Approximate resultant shapes for raglan extending into yoke

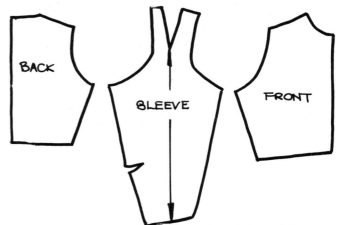

Fig. 7.34 Approximate resultant shapes for raglan extending into yoke.

Approximate resultant shapes for saddle shoulder
Fig. 7.35
Now follow stages 5–9 previously described in fitted sleeve with elbow dart.

Fig. 7.35 Approximate resultant shapes for saddle shoulder.

An alternative method for achieving a high raglan sleeve

Tape your stand – centre front, centre back, neckline side seam, waistline, shoulder and raglan style line desired.

Select and prepare your material – for the bodice and the sleeve. Using the basic modelled sleeve block, cut sleeve out in muslin as far as the underarm point, leaving a wide area above, enough to reach the neckline in length and centres in width.

Place and pin material onto stand in the following way

Model the bodice as far as the taped raglan line.

Pin the taped arm to the stand, allowing it to lie against the torso, then model the sleeve around the arm as far as the underarm point.

Smooth the fabric round the taped style lines; pin and cut away surplus. Smooth fabric to the shoulder seam; pin and cut away surplus.

Now follow stages 4–9 previously described in fitted sleeve with elbow darts.

SLEEVES CUT ALL-IN-ONE WITH BODICE

Sleeves cut all-in-one with the bodice have been used for thousands of years. Such sleeves, whilst giving ease under the arm, do have the tendency to drag over the shoulder.

(1) Classic kimono/magyar sleeve

Stage 1. Prepare the stand

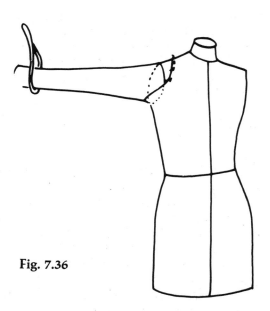

Fig. 7.36

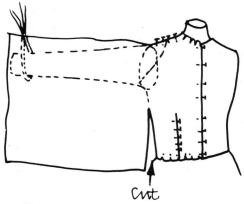

Fig. 7.37

Fig. 7.36

Pin the arm onto the stand as previously described.

Tie a tape round the wrist and attach to an immovable object so that the arm is suspended. The amount of ease under the arm increases the more the arm is raised, and conversely, the length from neck to wrist is decreased.

Stage 2. Tape your stand

On all kimono styles, the side seam, shoulder seam and underarm seam are centralised, i.e. are placed halfway between the centre back and front and front waist and back waist lengthwise.

Tape – neckline, centre front, centre back, shoulders, waist and any style lines, sleeve length and new centre line of sleeve (extension of shoulder line down arm).

Stage 3. Select and prepare material as previously described

Allow enough material in width to accommodate arm length.

Stage 4. Place and pin material onto stand in the following way

Fig. 7.37

Front. Pin lengthwise grain down centre of stand, allowing enough material above and below stand to accommodate the style. Model bodice in the normal way as previously described as far as the shoulder point and the side seam at waist level. (*Note:* the underarm point can be lowered to any depth provided the wrist level of the sleeve does not fall below the waist level of the stand.)

Cut away surplus fabric up to underarm point.

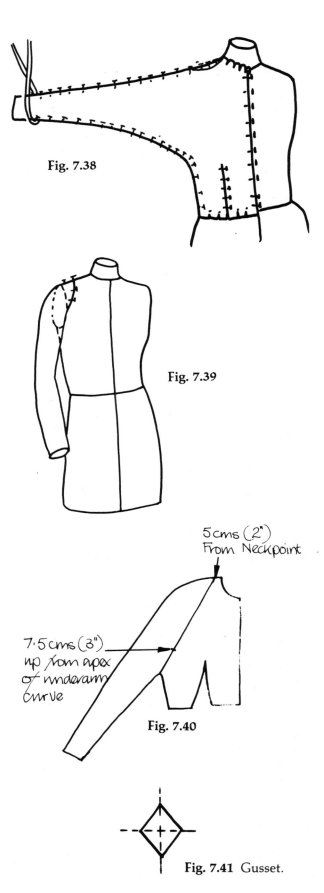

Fig. 7.38

Fig. 7.39

5 cms (2")
From Neckpoint

7·5 cms (3")
up from apex
of underarm
curve

Fig. 7.40

Fig. 7.41 Gusset.

Fig. 7.38

Smooth fabric along shoulder seam and down arm. Pin to taped shoulder line and arm. Cut away surplus fabric to within 1 cm (½"). Pin fabric at wrist and waist in line with taped seam and cut away to desired shape.

Back. Follow the same procedure as for front, then pin back and front along the underarm seam.

Stage 5. Mark in all details and remove from stand.

Stage 6. Press.

Stage 7. True all lines and check details.

Stage 8. Check seam allowances.

Stage 9. Make up and press.

Stage 10. Place on stand and check for any discrepancies.

(2) Fitted kimono/magyar sleeve with gusset

Prepare the stand

Fig. 7.39

Pin the arm onto the stand and suspend as previously described. This style gives a more fitted effect since the arm can be lowered below the waist level. A gusset is necessary to allow for ease. Here the underarm measurement has decreased and the measurement from neck to wrist has increased.

Tape your stand – as for classic kimono.

Select and prepare your material as previously described

Allow enough material to accommodate sleeve length below waist level.

Stage 4. Place and pin material onto stand in the following way

Fig. 7.40

The procedure for this sleeve with a gusset is the same as that for a classic kimono sleeve, but when the toile is removed from the stand, draw a line from the apex of the underarm curve to approximately 5 cms (2") from the neckpoint on the shoulder. Mark in this line for 7.5 cms (3") up from underarm.

Fig. 7.41

The gusset is inserted with a minimum seam allowance.

The gusset is cut on the true bias to give maximum stretch and on the double to give maximum strength. It is cut to a size of approximately 10 cms × 12.5 cms (4" × 5").

Other gussets may be incorporated into a kimono block, such as a strip gusset which is a panel extending from waist to end of sleeve, or a shortened strip gusset.

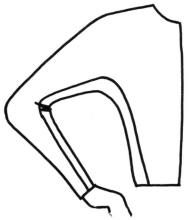

Fig. 7.42 Strip gusset.

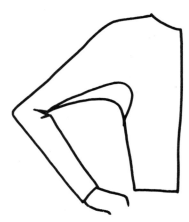

Fig. 7.43 Shortened strip gusset.

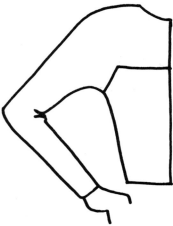

Fig. 7.44 Gusset incorporated into a yoke.

Figs. 7.42, 7.43 and 7.44
Gussets may also be incorporated into a yoke (see styles in Figs. 7.42, 7.43 and 7.44) by increasing the angle at underarm style lines.

Back

Follow the same procedure as for the front.

Half set-in kimono/magyar sleeve

An alternative method of producing a closely-fitted sleeve all-in-one with bodice, is by the introduction of a seam from the armhole into a princess line. The half set-in kimono sleeve is set in at the underarm for approximately 7.5 cms (3″) into a side panel, whilst the sleeve is all-in-one with the bodice along the shoulders.

Fig. 7.45
Tape the Stand
(*Note:* For this style, the arm is not pinned to the stand until the side panel has been modelled.)

Tape armhole, neckline, centre front, centre back, shoulders, waist, side panel style line (the front style line should pass over the bust), side seam (the underarm point should be lowered as desired).
Select and prepare your material as previously described
Place and pin side panel material onto stand in the following way

Fig. 7.46
Model the side panels back and front as for a princess line basic block as previously described in Chapter 2.

Lowered Underarm Point

Fig. 7.45

Side Panel Modelled Before Attaching Arm

Fig. 7.46 Side panels are modelled back and front before attaching arm.

For front and back centre panels allow enough material in depth to accommodate the length of sleeve.
Prepare your side panel material separately.
Pin arm onto stand

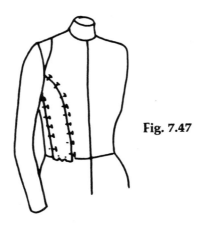

Fig. 7.47

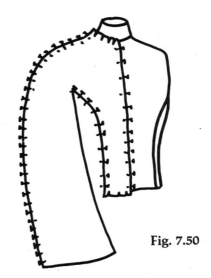

Fig. 7.49

Fig. 7.47
Pin arm onto stand as previously described allowing the arm to fall naturally, i.e. it will swing slightly forward and lie close to the stand.
Place and pin front and back centre panel onto stand in the following way

Fig. 7.49
Smooth out to princess line as far as armhole.
   Pin down princess line and cut away surplus to within 1 cm (½″).

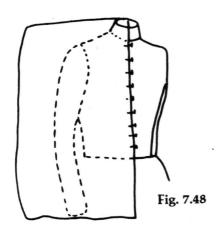

Fig. 7.48

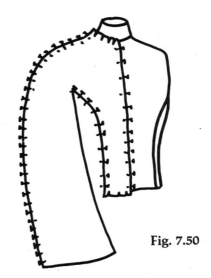

Fig. 7.50

Centre panel

Fig. 7.48
Pin warp grain of fabric onto centre front line allowing enough fabric above neck and below waist to accommodate the sleeve.

Fig. 7.50
Smooth fabric round neck, nick and cut away surplus to within 1 cm (½″).
   Continue along taped shoulder line down arm to wrist.
   Pin and cut away surplus to within 1 cm (½″).

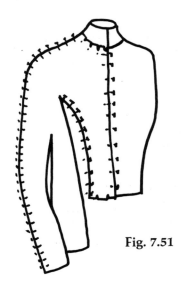

Fig. 7.51

Fig. 7.51
Smooth fabric round wrist to taped underarm.
　Smooth fabric round onto taped underarm seam as far as underarm point.

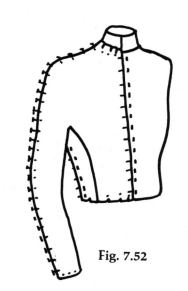

Fig. 7.52

Fig. 7.52
Smooth fabric round onto taped underarm seam of the side panel and pin. Smooth, pin and cut away surplus fabric along waistline to princess line.
　Pin cut away surplus fabric to desired shape.

Centre back panel

Repeat procedure for centre back panel and pin along underarm seam.
Mark in all details and remove from stand
Press
True all lines and check details
Check seam allowances
Place on stand and check for any discrepancies

(3) The dolman sleeve

The dolman or batwing sleeve has a low armhole (sometimes down to waist level) with maximum folds under the arm.
Prepare your stand

Fig. 7.53
Pin the arm onto the stand and suspend as previously described, allowing the arm to be raised to a level above the neck.
Tape your stand – as for a classic kimono.
Select and prepare your material as previously described
Allow enough material above the level of the neck for the sleeve length.
Place and pin material onto stand in the following way

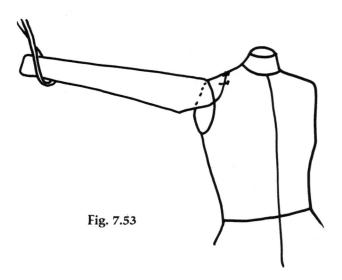

Fig. 7.53

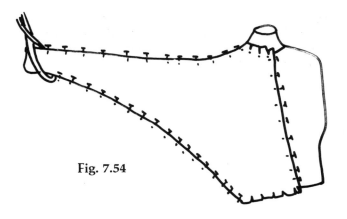

Fig. 7.54

Fig. 7.54
Model as for a classic kimono, but sleeve will fit tightly at wrist and have full drapes under the arm.

Back

Follow the same procedure as the front. Now follow stages 5–10 for the classic kimono previously described.

Variations of the kimono

A variety of styles may be achieved using the various procedures as described, by adding seam lines (see examples in Fig. 7.55).

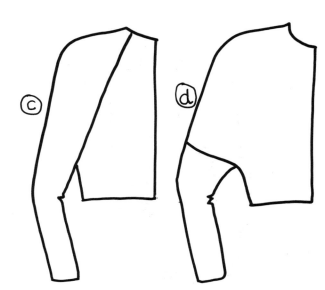

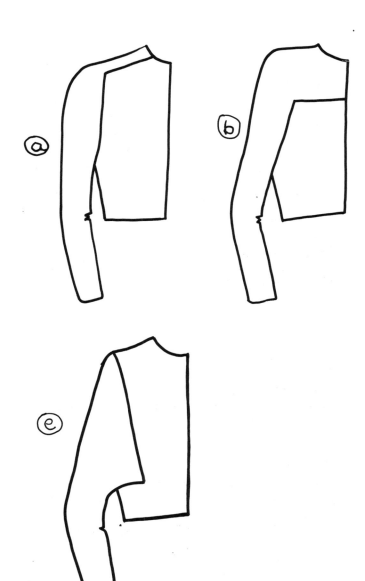

Fig. 7.55 Variations of the kimono. (a) Low saddle. (b) Yoke and sleeve combined. (c) Deep raglan. (d) Low dropped shoulder. (e) Low square armhole.

CHAPTER 8
DRAPED STYLES

INTRODUCTION

Throughout the text we have referred to the shaping of fabric around the dress stand as modelling rather than the alternative term – draping – in order not to confuse the reader when following this section. The term draping as used here is referring to a *type of styling*. The styles illustrated are classical and exemplify the principles underlying the manipulation of draped styles.

There are some fabrics which lend themselves more readily to draped styles because they have a quality which allows the material to hang in unison with and complementary to the body. In other words they possess 'drape'. Examples of such fabrics are jersey, chiffon and moss crepe.

Draped styles are those which accommodate the material in achieving the desired effect. Using the procedures described below, you will find that greater freedom of expression in your design is possible.

DRAPING ON THE STAND

One of the main advantages of this technique is that by experimenting in draping material onto the stand, you can build up a desired effect before cutting into the fabric. The illustrative stage of design can be delayed until after the experimental stage, the illustration, in effect, being a record of the artistry displayed on the stand.

General procedure

Stage 1. Drape the uncut length of dress fabric over the stand
If the garment is for an individual client or yourself, first drape the uncut length of your fabric on the figure. This will enable you to evaluate the colouring and posture of the individual with the fabric and the line of the drapes.

Drape the fabric on the stand for the overall effect. Observe its natural characteristics, i.e. the way it falls, its handle, texture and weight etc. Experimentation can now take place. Do not cut

into the fabric, but pin to hold where necessary. Aim for the overall effect; details can be worked out later. Note, first of all, the silhouette. Since each fabric drapes in a different way, this in turn alters the silhouette. Drapery is best continuing in line rather than as a separate piece, although this is not easily achieved. Alternative ideas may develop at this experimental stage. Evaluate your details. For example, checks or stripes placed on various grains will give different effects. Tucks may look better than gathers in certain fabrics. If you intend to use trimmings, place them onto the fabric to see how well they coordinate.

Stage 2. Substitute dress fabrics
To model the entire garment in the actual fabric is ideal, but unfortunately it makes experimentation expensive. For this reason, professional designers may use a fabric with similar properties which has been left over from a previous collection. Alternatively, the non-draped parts of the garment can be modelled in muslin with just the draped sections made in the actual fabric. When draping designs for checks or stripes, mark in the position of the lines on the muslin to get the effect of the fabric and to match the lines along the seams.

Stage 3. Tape your stand
Centre front, centre back, shoulders, seamlines, style lines, necklines, waist, hip and bustline and position and direction of drapes. (The horizontal and vertical balance lines help the drapes to hang correctly.)

If the fabric is not transparent you will not be able to see the taped lines below it, therefore sink pins along the taped lines, the pin heads below the fabric being your guide.

Stage 4. Select and prepare your material
The preparation of garment material is as previously described. A whole garment is cut, therefore allow enough material to cover both sides of the stand for each section.

When estimating the amount needed for draped styles, bear in mind that extra fabric will be required for the drawing up of folds from the bottom, down from the top and the depth of the fold itself. The more exaggerated the design, the more fabric needs to be allowed. Ideally, the draping quality of the warp and weft grain should be the same in order to match both sides of a drape. Allow plenty of excess material beyond the outer edges of the stand and mark in the centre vertical line and the warp grain with a contrasting thread.

As you become more experienced you will recognise roughly the size and shape required for certain results.

Stage 5. Place and pin material onto the stand in the following way
A full toile is required, but you need to model one side only, except for asymmetric designs where both sides must be modelled. If translating any draped styles from a sketch, observe where the folds are coming from and going to and the amount involved at either end.

Fig. 8.1
Line up the vertical central thread with the centre front line of the stand and pin. To avoid injury to the fabric, use very fine pins, e.g. silk pins, and keep pinning to a minimum. Temporarily pin the surplus fabric to the side of the stand you are not modelling.

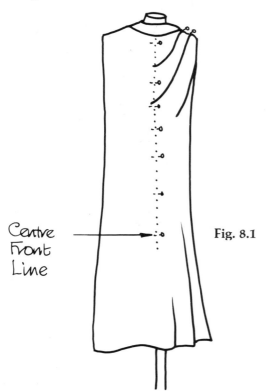

Centre
Front
Line   Fig. 8.1

Mould the fabric around the stand as desired, allowing the excess fabric to fall freely into the area where you wish the fullness of the drape to be placed. Use drapes in place of darts. The drapes can be continued along the outer edges of the stand and be allowed to fall forwards or backwards into a cascade of drapery, or be caught up into a seam line etc. Use the grain to experiment for the best effect, remembering that fabric drapes best on the bias.

It is sometimes necessary to control drapes, e.g. on a wide neckline where the neckline could fall off the shoulders, or, in the case of side panels, where billows might occur. The following methods are used to control drapes:

(a) by mounting the drapes on a fitted section, in which case, the fitted section should be modelled first;
(b) by weights placed inside the drapes;
(c) by taping.

Stage 6. Indicate all details
All the details should be indicated with pins rather than chalk and the pins should follow the direction of any darts, tucks, seams, etc.

Stage 7. Remove from stand

Stage 8. Press
Do not press over pins as they will leave an impression in the fabric.

Stage 9. True all lines and check details
The rough design now needs to be trued in order to establish the correct grainline and to ensure that the armhole, underarm seams and shoulders are the same length both sides – although perhaps not the same shape on the left and right side if the design is asymmetric.

When a symmetric full toile is modelled, the left and right side will not be exactly the same. Therefore, choose the better side and fold that side over on the centre line on the double to transfer shape and details. Transfer all markings with thread.

Stage 10. Check seam allowances

Stage 11. Make up and press

Stage 12. Place on stand or model and check for any discrepancies

(A) DRAPED STYLES DEVELOPED FROM EXTENSIONS BEYOND OUTER EDGES

At the experimental stage, a variety of designs can occur by playing about with excess fabric beyond the outer edges of the garment, either as a detail, or for the overall effect of the garment. Let your ideas flow freely, using off-cuts of material so that you are not restricted by having to cut into expensive fabric. Many alternative details develop as you proceed.

Ideas from extensions beyond outer edges of a garment

Figure 8.2 illustrates some ideas.

Fig. 8.2

(B) DRAPED STYLES DEVELOPED BY SLASHING AND LOWERING THE GRAIN

Fig. 8.3
A further development in the use of excess fabric beyond the seam edge is to slash into a point of intersection within the garment. An endless variety of details can develop without any preconceived plan. The fabric will fall into a circular flare as you slash from beyond a seam at any point towards any intersection. Some examples are shown in Fig. 8.3.

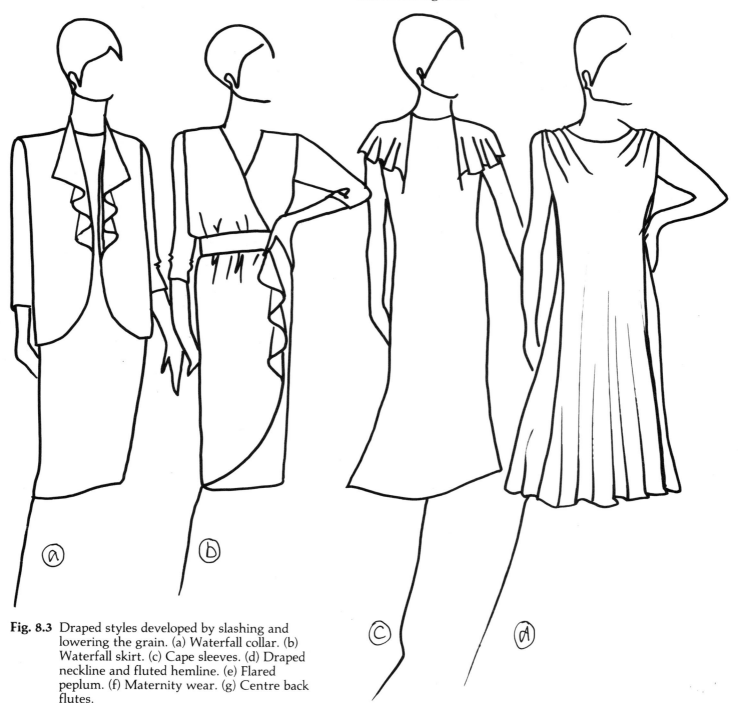

Fig. 8.3 Draped styles developed by slashing and lowering the grain. (a) Waterfall collar. (b) Waterfall skirt. (c) Cape sleeves. (d) Draped neckline and fluted hemline. (e) Flared peplum. (f) Maternity wear. (g) Centre back flutes.

General procedure

Fig. 8.4

Leave as much excess material as possible beyond the edge of the section of the garment where you wish drapes to occur. Model the section smoothing the fabric towards the draped area. Slash in from the excess fabric to the point of intersection. This will release fabric for you to arrange your drapes as desired with the excess fabric.

When slashing into the main body of the garment, it is sometimes necessary to insert an extension under the drapery to act as a support for the adjoining part of the garment (see following example (3)).

As can be seen from the following illustrations, many draped design ideas can be achieved using this method. A further stage in development is in allowing the grain to be lowered at points along a seam line to repeat the flares.

(1) Slash along shoulder to intersection of neck and shoulder

An example of this method can produce a 'waterfall collar'.

Procedure

Fig. 8.5

Tape your stand – centre front, centre back, side seam, waist, hip and bust lines, shoulder seam, armhole and desired style.
Select and prepare your material as previously described

Allow plenty of material above neckline and beyond centre front to accommodate waterfall draping.

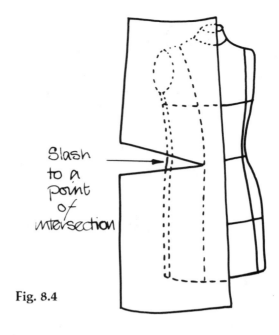

Fig. 8.4

Place and pin material onto stand in the following way

Fig. 8.6

Leave extension beyond shoulder, neck and centre front and pin lengthwise grain down centre front. Model bodice as desired, placing a pin at intersection point.

Slash along shoulder line from shoulder point to neck and shoulder intersection where pin has been placed.

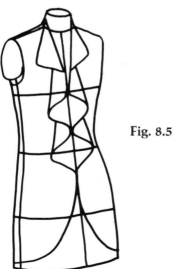

Fig. 8.5

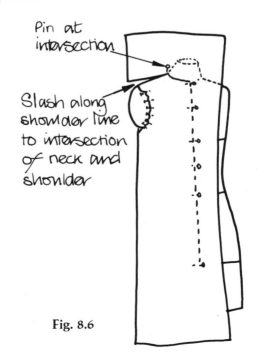

Fig. 8.6

Slash opened and grain lowered

Fig. 8.7

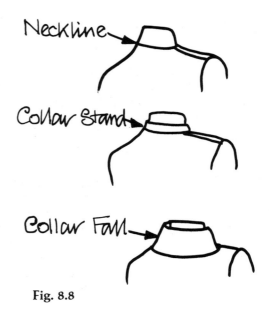

Neckline

Collar Stand

Collar Fall

Fig. 8.8

Fig. 8.7
Using your right hand to lower the grain will cause the slash to open and drapes to form.

The more the grain is lowered, the more drapes will appear.

Lower the grain until the desired amount of draping is achieved.

Hold drapes temporarily with a few pins under the drapes and push the upper edge of the slash round the back neck and pin along back neckline.

Fig. 8.8
Check the design. The drapes may

(i)   end at the shoulder/neck intersection;
(ii) be smoothed round along the back neckline to the centre back and taken into a collar stand; or
(iii) be allowed to roll over into a collar along the back of the neck.

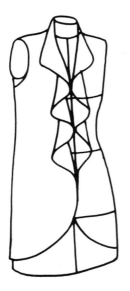

Fig. 8.9
Cut lower edges of drape to desired shape.

Model back as desired.

Now follow stages 6–12 previously described in this chapter.

Fig. 8.9

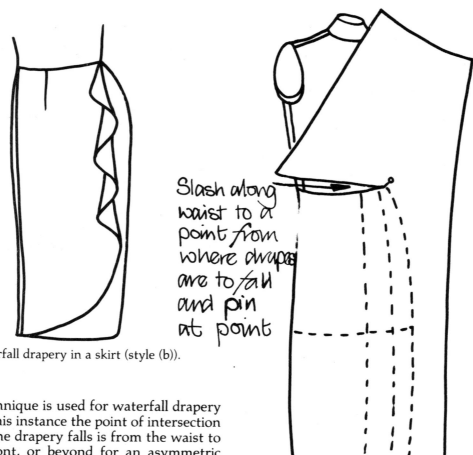

Slash along waist to a point from where drapes are to fall and pin at point

Fig. 8.10 Waterfall drapery in a skirt (style (b)).

Fig. 8.10
The same technique is used for waterfall drapery in a skirt. In this instance the point of intersection from where the drapery falls is from the waist to the centre front, or beyond for an asymmetric effect.

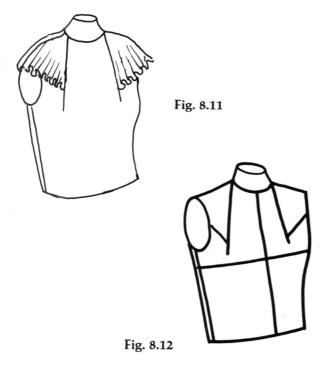

Fig. 8.11

Fig. 8.12

(2) Slash into neck dart at intersection of neck and shoulder

An example of this method can produce a flared frill along the shoulder line extending into the neck dart (Fig. 8.11).

Procedure

Fig. 8.12
Tape your stand – centre front, centre back, side seam, waistline, bustline, dart position, shoulder seam, armhole and line for desired depth of frill.
Select and prepare your material as previously described
   Allow plenty of material above neckline and shoulder line to allow for frill.
Place and pin material onto stand in the following way

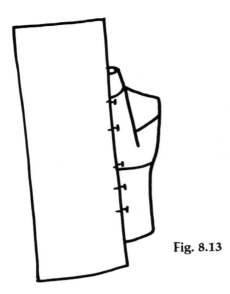

Fig. 8.13

Fig. 8.13
Leave extension beyond shoulder and neck, then pin lengthwise edge of fabric down centre front.

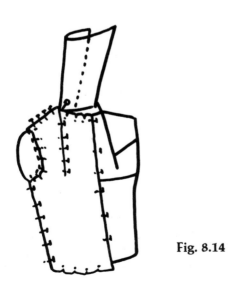

Fig. 8.14

Fig. 8.14
Model bodice as for basic block with dart from neck/shoulder intersection, but leave surplus dart fullness uncut beyond the neckline.

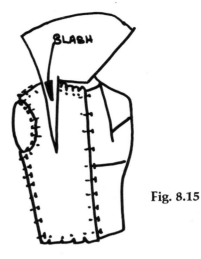

Fig. 8.15

Fig. 8.15
Slash from the neck/shoulder intersection on the shoulder line through to the centre of the neck dart, on the side of the dart nearest to the shoulder.

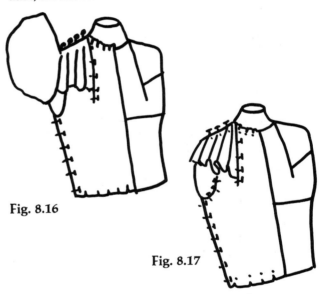

Fig. 8.16

Fig. 8.17

Figs. 8.16 and 8.17
Lower the grain, pin onto shoulder 1 cm (½″) away from neck edge. Cut away surplus fabric to within 1 cm (½″). Continue in the same way until the end of the shoulder is reached. As the grain is lowered, flares will form. Those nearest to the neck dart can be pushed into the dart towards the centre front. Cut desired shape on the lower edge of the flare.

Model back as desired.

Now follow stages 6–12 previously described in this chapter.

Further styles may be achieved by the same process. It can be taken a stage further by allowing the flare to continue round the back or down the sleeve, in a variety of ways.

(3) Slash from side seam along waist to centre front

Fig. 8.18 Draped neckline and fluted skirt.

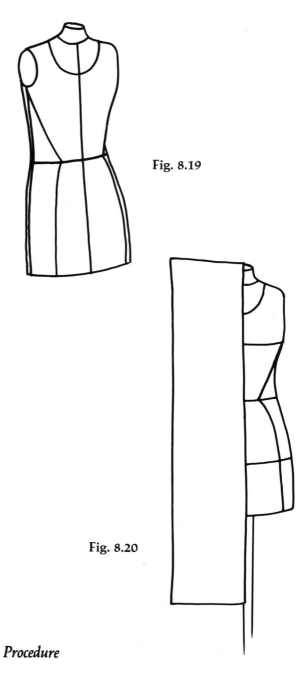

Fig. 8.19

Fig. 8.20

Fig. 8.18
The procedure shown is for the centre panel. Side panels are modelled as for basic blocks.

Procedure

Fig. 8.19
Tape your stand – centre front, hipline, waistline, side seam, style line, neckline, shoulder seam, armhole.
Select and prepare your material as previously described
    Leave plenty of material beyond the sides of the stand.
Place and pin material onto stand in the following way

Fig. 8.20
Pin lengthwise edge of fabric to centre front, making sure a pin is placed at waist level.

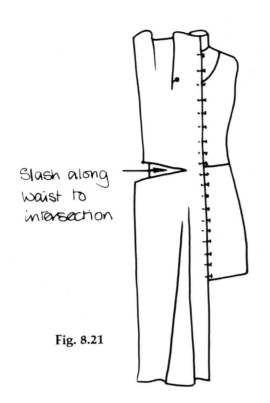

Slash along waist to intersection

Fig. 8.21

Fig. 8.21
Slash into fabric from sides along waistline as far as intersection. Temporarily pin upper half to stand.

Fig. 8.22
Lower grain along style line of skirt, pinning every 1 cm (½″) and placing flares in position. Cut away surplus to within 1 cm (½″). Continue in the same way until hem is reached.

Fig. 8.23
Repeat the process for the bodice section but raising the grain, until the shoulder/armhole intersection is reached and then arrange fullness at shoulder or neckline or both into desired style.

Now mould plain side section as for skirt and bodice to fill the gap created by lowering and raising the grain for flares and drapes.

Model back as desired.

Now follow stages 6–12 previously described in this chapter.

Further styles may be achieved by the same process. Flares can be achieved along the back.

Figure 8.24 shows flares being taken to the side seam of a peplum.

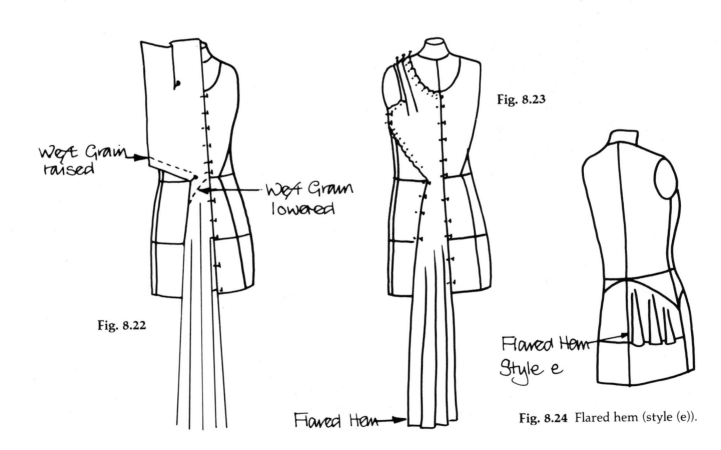

Weft Grain raised

Weft Grain lowered

Fig. 8.22

Fig. 8.23

Flared Hem

Flared Hem Style e

Fig. 8.24 Flared hem (style (e)).

(4) Slash from diagonal slash to below bust point

High waisted styles suitable for maternity wear (Fig. 8.25) can also be achieved by having the intersection point around bust level.

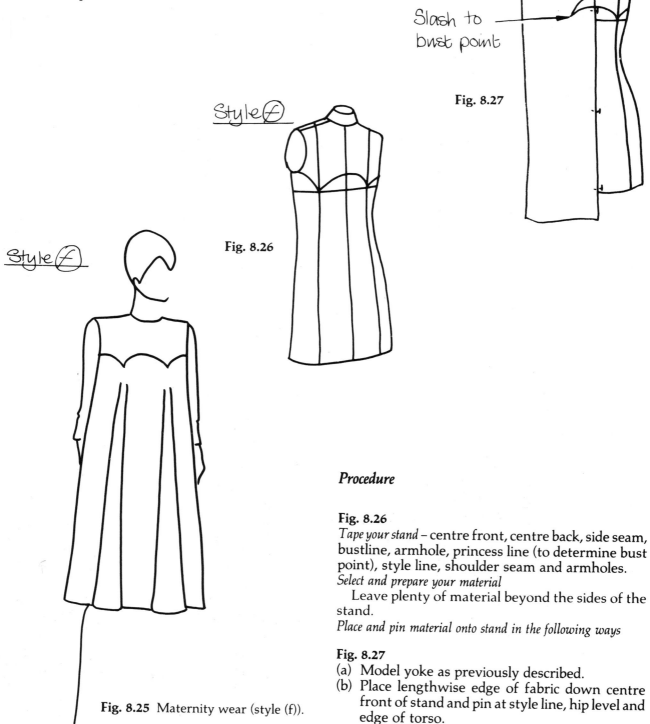

Slash to bust point

Fig. 8.27

Style (f)

Fig. 8.26

Style (f)

Fig. 8.25 Maternity wear (style (f)).

Procedure

Fig. 8.26
Tape your stand – centre front, centre back, side seam, bustline, armhole, princess line (to determine bust point), style line, shoulder seam and armholes.
Select and prepare your material
   Leave plenty of material beyond the sides of the stand.
Place and pin material onto stand in the following ways

Fig. 8.27
(a) Model yoke as previously described.
(b) Place lengthwise edge of fabric down centre front of stand and pin at style line, hip level and edge of torso.
   Slash along style line from centre front to bust point intersection

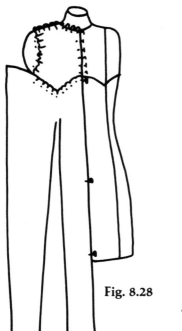

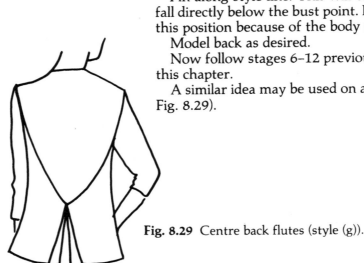

Fig. 8.28
Lower the grain until cut edge reaches other side of style line.

Pin along style line. This will cause the flare to fall directly below the bust point. It can only fall in this position because of the body contour.

Model back as desired.

Now follow stages 6–12 previously described in this chapter.

A similar idea may be used on a back jacket (see Fig. 8.29).

Fig. 8.28

Fig. 8.29 Centre back flutes (style (g)).

(5) Slash into main body then wind round body

In some cases it is necessary to slash into the main body of the garment from the extension before draping the extension around the body in order to change the direction of the folds. The styles illustrated in Figs. 8.30, 8.31 and 8.32 exemplify this. In all these styles the fullness is pushed towards the centre front then slashed from the outer edges from the direction of the folds towards the bust point. The extension is then wound round the contours as desired. We shall choose the style in Fig. 8.32 as our example to show the technique.

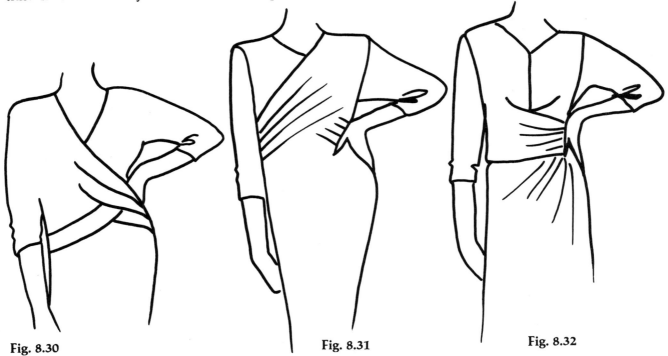

Fig. 8.30   **Fig. 8.31**   **Fig. 8.32**

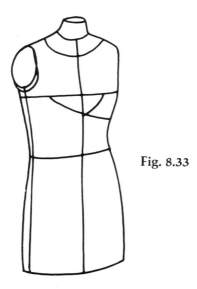

Fig. 8.33

Procedure for style in Fig. 8.32

Fig. 8.33
Tape your stand – centre front, centre back, sideseam, waist, neckline, bustline, shoulder seam, armhole and draped line.

Select and prepare your material
Leave plenty of material beyond the side of the stand where you wish the drapes to occur.
Place and pin material onto stand in the following way

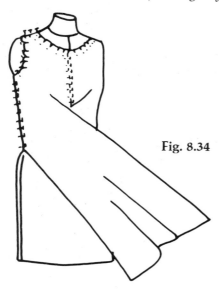

Fig. 8.34

Fig. 8.34
A whole toile is modelled for this asymmetric design. Model bodice as previously described as far as side seam/waist intersection, pushing excess fullness to centre front near waist. Slash from outer edge towards bust point in the direction you wish the drapes to occur.

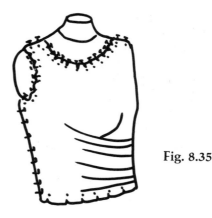

Fig. 8.35

Fig. 8.35
Wind surplus fabric round waist and either pin into side seam or, if extension is long enough, take round back waist to other side seam. Pin and cut away surplus. Model back as desired. Now follow stages 6–12 previously described in this chapter.

(C) DRAPED STYLES DEVELOPED BY SLASHING AND GATHERING OR TUCKING

Previously, we slashed the excess fabric then lowered the grain to produce flares. Now, having made your slash or slashes freely instead of lowering the grain, gather or tuck the extension into folds.

Style (a)

Fig. 8.36 (style (a)).

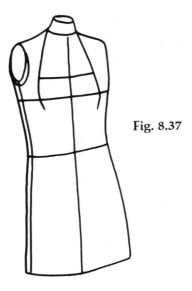

Fig. 8.37

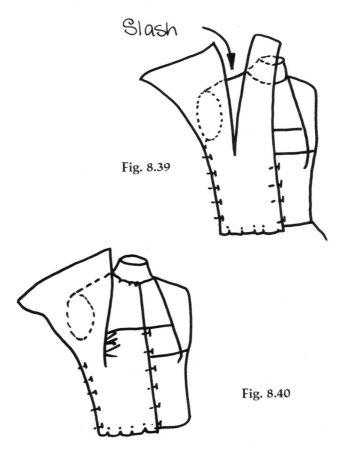

Slash

Fig. 8.39

Fig. 8.40

Procedure

Fig. 8.37
Tape your stand – centre front, centre back, shoulders, waistline, neckline, style lines, bustline, armhole, side seams.

Select and prepare your material
Allow enough material to extend beyond centre front for gathers, and beyond shoulder line for folds.
Place and pin material onto stand in the following way

Figs. 8.39 and 8.40
Slash from neck/shoulder intersection to just below bust point; place and pin gathers along cut edge nearest to centre front onto taped styleline. Cut to neckline. Place and pin folds along shoulder line to neck as desired.

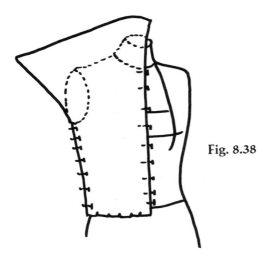

Fig. 8.38

Fig. 8.38
Model bodice as previously described, pushing excess towards neck/shoulder intersection. Model as far as underarm/side seam intersection.

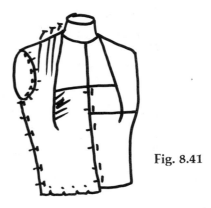

Fig. 8.41

Fig. 8.41
Model around armhole and cut away surplus and pin.
   Model back as desired.
   Now follow stages 6–12 previously described in this chapter.

Style (b)

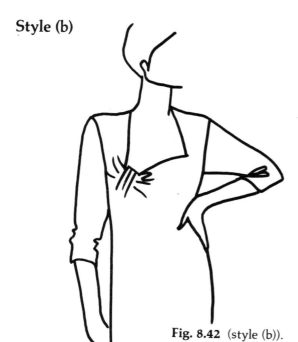

Fig. 8.42 (style (b)).

Asymmetric styles may also be achieved by the same process, but a full toile will be required. An example of an asymmetric style is shown in Fig. 8.42. The technique is set out below.

Procedure

Fig. 8.43

Fig. 8.43
Tape your stand – centre front, centre back, shoulders, waistline, neckline, style lines, bustline, armhole, sideseams.
Select and prepare your material
  Allow enough material for extension beyond arm-holes, shoulders and neckline for a whole front.
Place and pin material onto stand in the following way

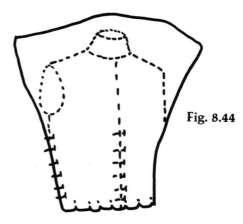

Fig. 8.44

Fig. 8.44
Model bodice as previously described, pushing excess towards neck/shoulder intersections.
  Model as far as armhole/sideseam intersections.

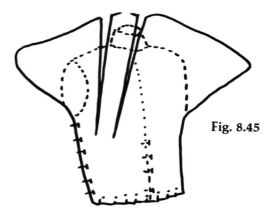

Fig. 8.45

Fig. 8.45
Slash along style lines from which gathers radiate.
  Arrange folds and push into seam lines and gathers.

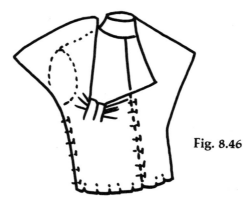

Fig. 8.46

Fig. 8.46
Cut away neckline to taped line on stand.

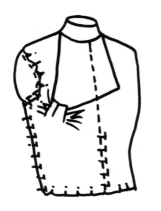

Fig. 8.47

Fig. 8.47
Model shoulders and armholes, cut away surplus and pin.

Model back as desired.

Now follow stages 6–12 as previously described in this chapter.

It is also possible to give a yoke effect (Fig. 8.48) by this method (see also Chapter 4 – Bodices).

Fig. 8.48

Leave plenty of fabric beyond centre front for gathering in.

(D) DRAPED STYLES DEVELOPED BY SLASHING AND FOLDING BACK EXTENSION ON ITSELF

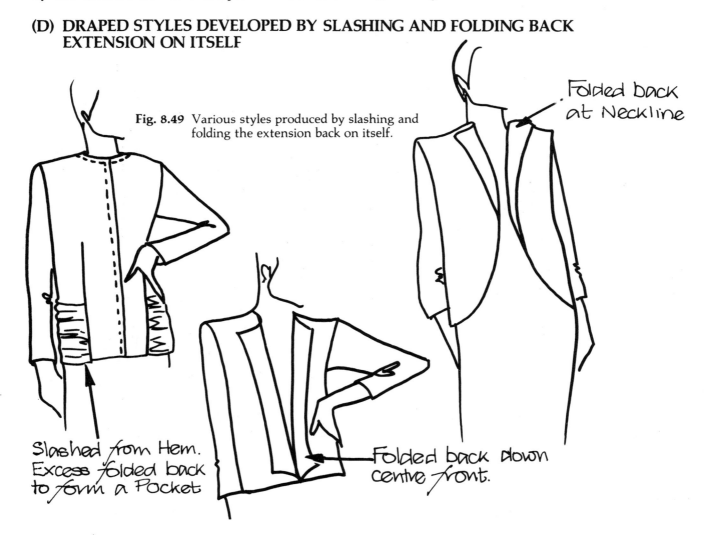

Fig. 8.49 Various styles produced by slashing and folding the extension back on itself.

Folded back at Neckline

Slashed from Hem. Excess folded back to form a Pocket

Folded back down centre front.

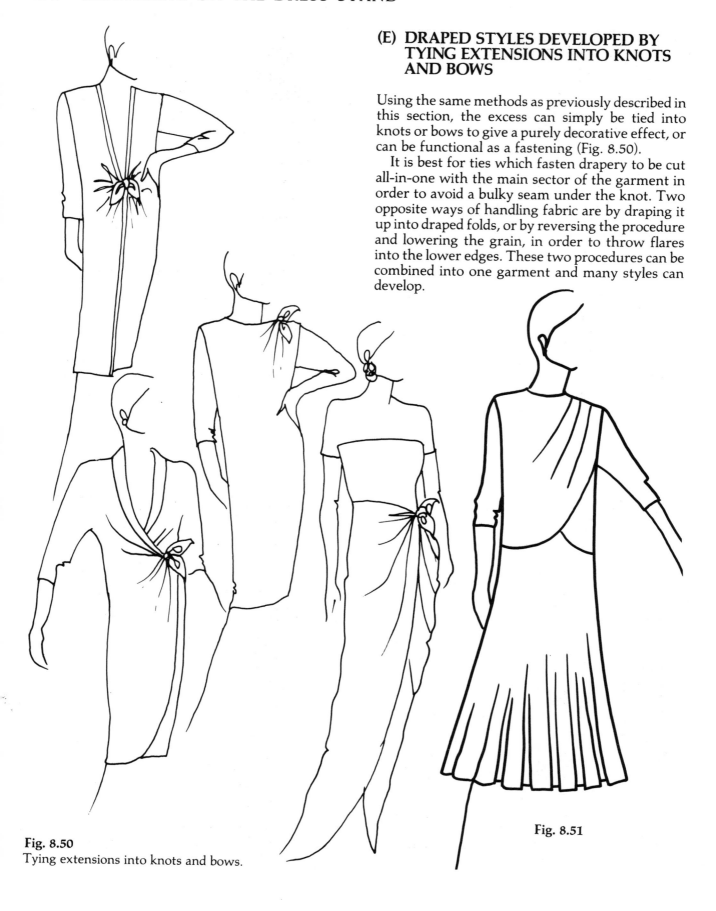

(E) DRAPED STYLES DEVELOPED BY TYING EXTENSIONS INTO KNOTS AND BOWS

Using the same methods as previously described in this section, the excess can simply be tied into knots or bows to give a purely decorative effect, or can be functional as a fastening (Fig. 8.50).

It is best for ties which fasten drapery to be cut all-in-one with the main sector of the garment in order to avoid a bulky seam under the knot. Two opposite ways of handling fabric are by draping it up into draped folds, or by reversing the procedure and lowering the grain, in order to throw flares into the lower edges. These two procedures can be combined into one garment and many styles can develop.

Fig. 8.50
Tying extensions into knots and bows.

Fig. 8.51

DRAPED STYLES BASED ON SIMPLE GEOMETRIC SHAPES, PAST AND PRESENT

Many draped styles are made from basic geometric shapes and have been utilised throughout history.

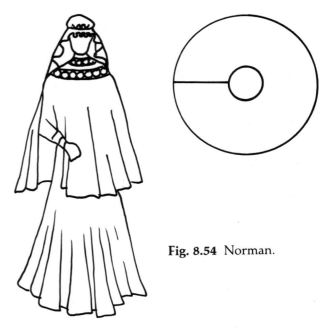

Fig. 8.54 Norman.

Norman – based on a circle with a hole in the centre, slit from neck to edge, then left undone in places to allow the free movement of one arm.

Fig. 8.52 Roman toga.

Roman toga – based on hexagon or circle. The circle is folded just about halfway.

Fig. 8.53 Saxon.

Saxon – based on a circle. The circle has a hole in the centre for the head to pass through.

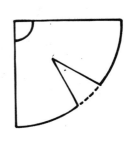

Fig. 8.55 Fifteenth century.

Fifteenth century – based on a circle but a wedge is cut in from the circumference, allowing a sleeve and bodice to be formed when sewn.

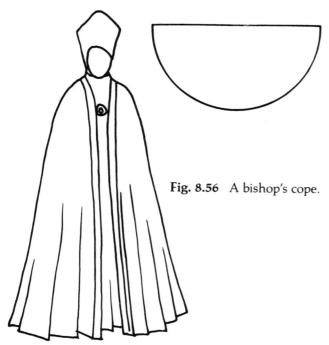

Fig. 8.56 A bishop's cope.

These historic geometric shapes can still be seen today. For example, a bishop's cope is based on a semi-circle (Fig. 8.56).

Fashionable dress during this century has utilised geometric shapes as a basis for design. Erté, foremost designer of original fashions at the beginning of this century, illustrated most complicated styles, but when analysed, it is clear they were based on geometric shapes.

Vionnet's famous handkerchief dress was based on four bias-cut squares, joined at the centre and sides. The outside edges then formed points which became shoulder straps and pointed hem (Fig. 8.57).

Fig. 8.57 Vionnet's 'handkerchief dress'.

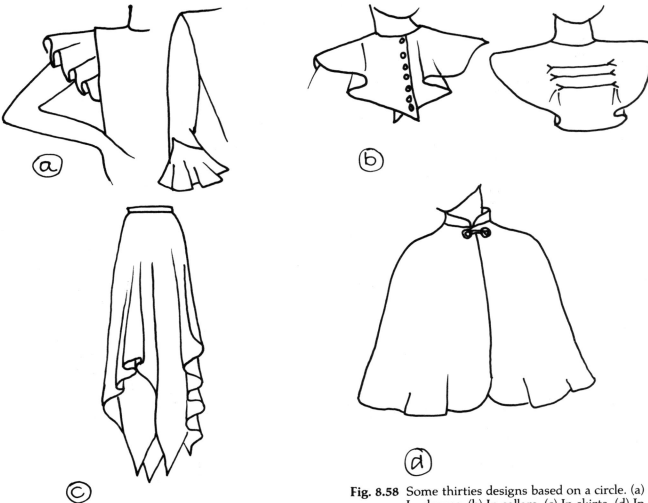

Figure 8.58 shows some thirties designs based on a circle and Fig. 8.59 shows some thirties designs based on a square.

Fig. 8.58 Some thirties designs based on a circle. (a) In sleeves. (b) In collars. (c) In skirts. (d) In capes.

Fig. 8.59 Some thirties collars designs based on a square.

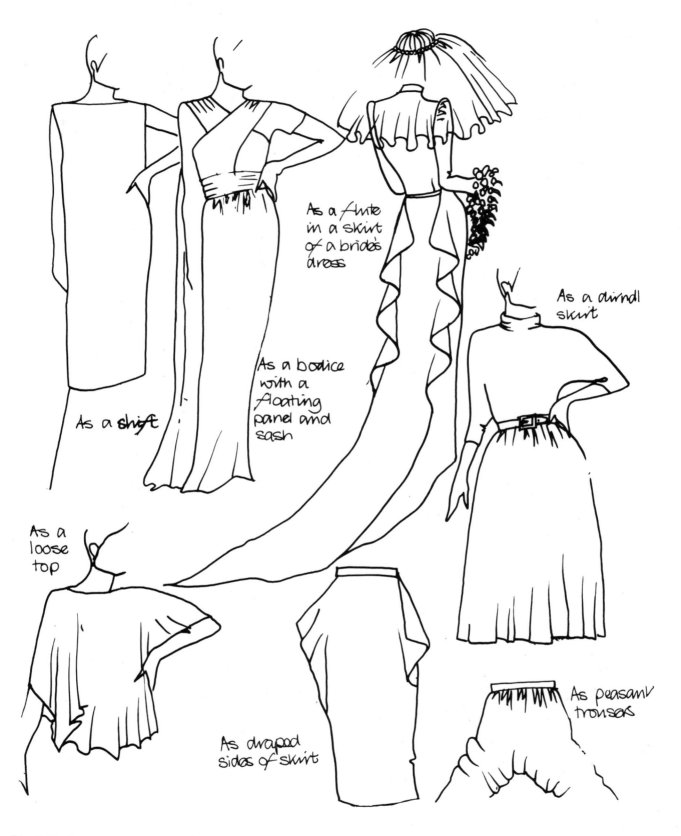

As a flute in a skirt of a bride's dress

As a bodice with a floating panel and sash

As a dirndl skirt

As a shift

As a loose top

As draped sides of skirt

As peasant trousers

Fig. 8.60 Some contemporary designs based on a rectangle.

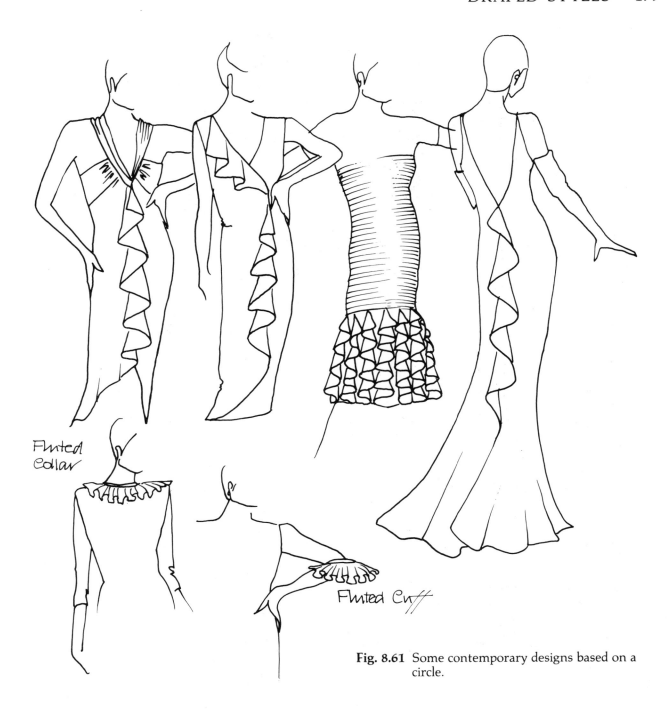

Flutea
Collar

Flutea Cuff

Fig. 8.61 Some contemporary designs based on a circle.

Geometric shapes in many dimensions are used today as the basis for designs. Figure 8.60 shows some examples based on a rectangle. A circle with a slit and central hole, when placed on a fairly straight seam, will give flutes as shown in Fig. 8.61. Some designs based on a triangle are shown in Fig. 8.62.

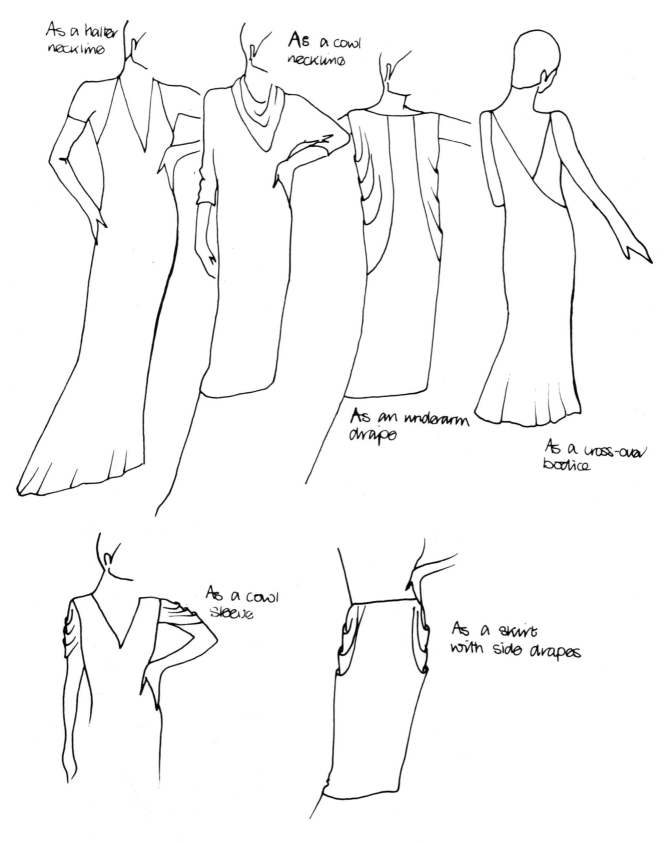

As a halter neckline

As a cowl neckline

As an underarm drape

As a cross-over bodice

As a cowl sleeve

As a skirt with side drapes

Fig. 8.62 Some designs based on a triangle.

CHAPTER 9
EXERCISE – A WEDDING DRESS

In order to bring together many of the skills expressed and developed in the previous chapters, the following exercise has been chosen.

Fig. 9.1
The design in question is quite obviously a wedding dress, but the procedure, with little alteration, could be used to produce a ball gown. If followed carefully, this exercise will demand levels of expertise which will test, in a most comprehensive way, your design and technical abilities.

(a)

(b)

(c)

Fig. 9.1 A wedding dress: (a) front; (b) back; (c) side.

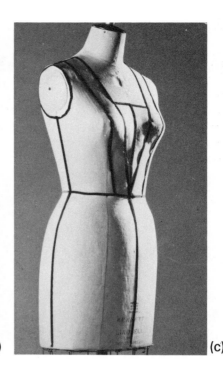

(a)   (b)   (c)

Fig. 9.2 Taping the stand: (a) front; (b) back; (c) side.

Stage 1: Tape the stand

Fig. 9.2
Tape the whole front and back torso for style lines, neck, shoulder, side seams, centre lines, waistline and armhole positions.

Taping the whole torso helps with judging the proportion of the style.

Stage 2: Model the front bodice on the right side

Fig. 9.3
Centre front panel
Mould the whole centre panel to taped lines, leaving large seam allowances on style line and 1 cm (½″) at neck and waist.

Middle front panel
Pin down centre of panel to position the grain.

Mould muslin to the contours of the torso within the taped lines.

Temporarily, pin away from the taped lines, then turn under seam allowances by creasing on the taped line towards the sides.

Let seam allowance at shoulder lie towards the back.

Pin perpendicularly across the seams.

Remove temporary pins.

Fig. 9.3 Modelling the front bodice on the right side.

Side front panel
Continue in same way as for the middle panel, but do not turn in the armhole seam allowances.

Pin muslin around the armholes as shown.

Stage 3: Back bodice

Fig. 9.4

Keeping the front bodice pinned to the stand, now model the back bodice in the same way. Temporarily, move pins 2.5 cm (1″) away from front side seam, in order to push back side seam allowances under, then repin perpendicularly across the side seam.

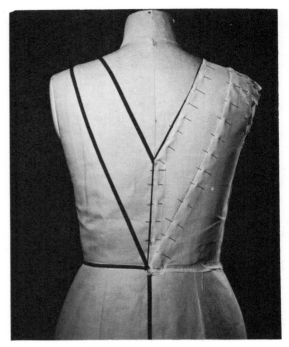

Fig. 9.4 Back bodice.

Stage 4: The collar

Fig. 9.5

Cut a long strip of muslin on the straight grain. This should be slightly wider than required and approximately 3 times the neck measurement from the centre front waist to centre back neck. Machine gather lengthwise on one side. Lay frill onto neckline and pin from centre front waistline along taped line to centre back neck. Shape outer edge as required.

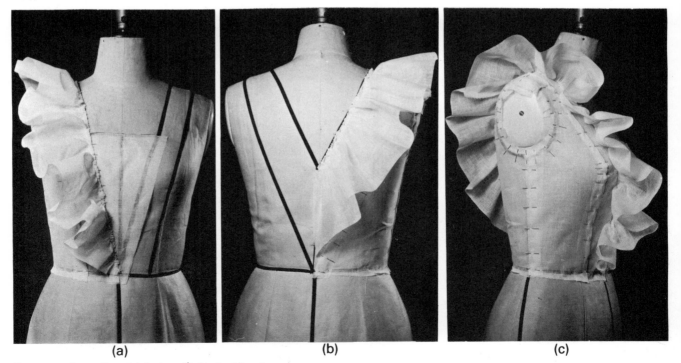

     (a)   (b)   (c)

Fig. 9.5 The collar: (a) front; (b) back; (c) side.

Fig. 9.6 The crinoline base.

Fig. 9.7 The underskirt.

Stage 5: The skirt

The underskirt

Figs. 9.6 and 9.7

Before the skirt is modelled a crinoline base skirt and underskirt are placed on the stand (the making up of this crinoline base is not dealt with as it can be purchased.) The underskirt is modelled in the same way as the dress skirt, but with less flare in the skirt and no gathers at the waist, or it can simply be bought ready-made.

The material used needs to be stiff and possibly starched. A strip of fabric is gathered onto the bottom, 3 times the distance round the hem of the underskirt by the depth required.

(Remember that circular skirts drop at the hemline, so it is advisable to hang the skirt for as long as possible before adding the frill.)

The skirt

Fig. 9.8

(For the sake of clarity, the skirt has been photographed without the crinoline.)

Raise or lower the stand to the wearer's height.

Fig. 9.8 The skirt.

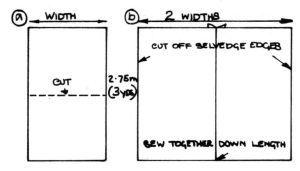

Fig. 9.9

Pin arm to torso underneath modelled bodice.

Fig. 9.10

Fig. 9.9
Take a 2.75 m (3 yd) length of muslin and cut in half across the length of muslin and cut in half across the length from selvedge to selvedge.

Cut off selvedge edges and sew the two pieces together lengthwise.

It may be necessary to join more pieces together. If this is so, the pieces must be joined on the straight grain, otherwise the pieces will stretch along the seam.

Place the bottom of the length to the floor, then pin at waist to hip down centre front.

Pin the waist at centre front.

Cut along for approximately 1 cm (½″) and place another pin easing fabric in for gathers.

Arrange flare, lowering the grain and pinning the waist. Cut away surplus fabric at waist to within 1 cm (½″) then nick into waist as you arrange each flare. Continue in the same manner until you reach the side seam.

This particular skirt has two full circles in it. The underskirt has one full circle in it.

In the first instance the warp grain lies down the centre front and sides. In the second instance the warp grain lies down the centre front and the weft grain lies down the sides.

In any case, the side seam should be perpendicular to the floor.

Back skirt

Leave the front skirt on the stand and model the back skirt in the same way.

When made up the skirt should be allowed to hang for as long as possible, then put back on the stand over the underskirts for the hem to be arranged.

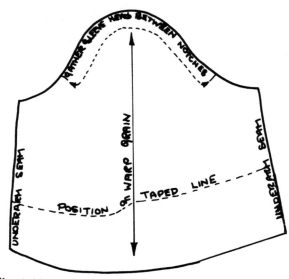

Fig. 9.11

Stage 6: The sleeve

Fig. 9.10
Pin arm to torso underneath modelled bodice.

Fig. 9.11
Using the full width of muslin, cut roughly the shape of the sleeve with the warp grain running lengthwise through the centre.

(a)

(b)

Fig. 9.12 The sleeve: (a) front; (b) side; (c) back.

Machine gather the sleeve head from approximately 10 cms (4") from the underarm seams.

Sew underarm seams together.

Press open.

On the flat, the sleeve shape from the underarm seam to 7.5 cms (3") up the sleeve head should be cut the same shape as the armhole curves on the front and back bodice.

Adjust the gathering around the sleeve head so that the sleeve head measurement equals that of the armhole.

Place the centre notch of the sleeve to shoulder seam. Place the underarm seam to side seam of bodice. Pin in.

Place tape tightly around the elbow line and arrange gathers, allowing sleeve to blouse over the tape. Mark in the taped line onto sleeve.

Arrange the length of sleeve and cut frill to shape.

Make a note of tape and size.

Mark in all seam lines and balance marks, then remove toile from stand.

(c)

INDEX

armhole, 95, 140-42
all-in-one basic shapes, 96-104
all-in-one collars, 132-6
all-in-one sleeves, 139, 150-55
arm, 140-42, 146

band collar, 128
bishop sleeve, 144
block, 7, 23, 65
blouse, 106
bodices, 65
   armholes, 95
   basic block, 65-7
   blouses, 105
   coats, 105
   darts, 69-78
   draped asymmetric, 91, 92
   flanges, 89
   gathers, tucks, pleats, 68
   internal seams, 79-83
   jackets, 105
   yokes, 84-8
   underarm cowl, 92-4
   waistlines, 95
buttons and button stand, 117

coats, 106
collars, 113-36
   all-in-one collar, 132-6
   basic principle, 113
   convertible collar, 128, 129
   flat, 114-17
   fluted, 118, 119
   rever, 130-32
   roll, 120-24
   stand, 125-9

darts, 69-78, 89, 90, 142, 143
dolman sleeve, 154, 155
draped styles
   from extensions, 159
   geometric shapes, 175-80

draped styles – *contd.*
   slashing and folding, 173
   slashing and gathering or tucking, 170-73
   slashing and lowering grain, 160-70
   tying and knotting, 174
drapes, 91-4, 157-80
dropped line, 104

Empire line, 104
equipment, 9
exercise — wedding dress, 181-6

fabric, 5, 21-3
flanges, 89, 90
flared sleeve, 144
flat collars, 114-17
flat pattern cutting, 5
fluted collars, 118-19

grain, 21, 22, 43, 44-6, 51, 160-70

half set-in sleeve, 152-4
high dropped shoulder, 147, 148

jackets, 106

kimonos
   classic, 150
   fitted with gusset, 151, 152

leg o' mutton sleeve, 144, 145

magyar sleeves, 150-55
mandarin collar, 126, 127
measurements, 10-17
modelling, 1

necklines, 107
   basic, 107
   cowl, 108-12

padding, 18, 19
peplum, 105
pinning, 24
pleats, 51, 68, 89, 90
princess line, 23-8, 100-104
puff sleeve, 145, 146

raglan high, 148-50
rever collar, 130-32
roll collar, 120-24

seams, 76, 79-83
skirts, 29
   bell-shaped, 36
   circular/flared, 41-8
   dirndl, 35, 36
   draped, 56-63
   draped asymmetric, 63
   draped peg-top, 57-60
   draped wrap-over, 61, 62
   gored, 43, 49-56
   plain straight, 31-3
   pleated, 37-40
   straight, 30
   straight wrap-over, 33, 34
   tiered, 37

sleeves, 137-55
   all-in-one, 139, 150
   bishop, 144
   dolman, 154, 155
   elbow dart, 142
   flared, 144
   half set-in, 152-4
   high drop shoulder, 147, 148
   high raglan, 148-50
   kimono, 150-55
   kimono classic, 150, 151
   kimono fitted with gusset, 151, 152
   leg o' mutton, 144, 145
   magyar, 150-55
   puff, 145, 146
   separate, 137, 138, 143-50
   wrist dart, 143
   wrist gathers, 143

stand collars, 125-9
stand cover, 23-8

taping, 19, 20
tucks, 51, 68, 77, 78, 89, 90, 170-73

waistline, 95
wedding dress, 181-6
wing collar, 128

yokes
   bodices, 84-8
   skirts, 39, 40